The Old Testament Experience of Faith

The Old Testament Experience of Faith

David T. Shannon

JUDSON PRESS ® VALLEY FORGE

THE OLD TESTAMENT EXPERIENCE OF FAITH

Library of Congress Cataloging in Publication Data

Shannon, David T.
    The Old Testament experience of faith.

    Includes bibliographical references.
    1. Bible. O. T.—History of Biblical events. 2. Christian life—Biblical teaching. I.
Title.
BS1197.S48   221.9'5   76-48512
ISBN 0-8170-0719-9

The name JUDSON PRESS is registered as a trademark in the U.S. Patent Office. Printed in the U.S.A. ⊕

"In the beginning God created . . ."
—Genesis 1:1

"Time does not become sacred to us until we have lived it."
—John Burroughs

Preface

The purpose of this book is to enable students and teachers to perceive the Bible as the Christian church's book of faith by examining the major developments in the Old Testament dramas and showing how they have been understood by the church as the basis for faith.

Specifically, the focus of this book will be the pivotal periods of Old Testament history, such as the formation of the nation, the Exile, and the return to Palestine. It is the author's assumption that the Old Testament grew out of the experiences of the Hebrew people—a set of individual and collective experiences not unlike those joys, trials, and ambiguities that are part of the human condition of every age, race, and religious persuasion. More importantly, this text cues us into the process of reflection of those experiences as the Hebrews struggled to wrench meaning and ultimate significance from what they observed happening to and around them.

The first chapter presents the three keys along with three critical questions, which will serve as guides to this study of the Old Testament.

Acknowledgments

The author has been assisted by many persons in the preparation of this manuscript, and it would be impossible to mention all of them by name because his indebtedness is great. However, several persons deserve special mention: Charles Oehrig and Eleanor Menke, who first invited the author to undertake this study and who have been a constant source of insight and inspiration during the entire production of this study; the assistance of Donald S. Gowan, Jared J. Jackson, and Eberhard von Waldow, colleagues in the area of Old Testament at Pittsburgh Theological Seminary, who read sections of the manuscript and made critical and helpful suggestions for the improvement of same; to the library staff at Pittsburgh Seminary, especially Betty Howard and Sally Seibel, who provided many hours of time in facilitating the use of the library in research and xeroxing; to Norma Caquatto, who read and edited the entire manuscript and made significant suggestions as to style and content; to my secretary, Clare Cashdollar, and Dorothy Dick, typists who prepared the manuscript. In addition to these persons just mentioned I must thank my wife, Averett, whose understanding, patience, and helpful insights added immeasurably to the preparation of the manuscript. Finally, I dedicate this book to my children, Vernitia, Davine, and David, Jr., who are seeking to learn more about the Bible as the church's book of faith.

DAVID T. SHANNON
PITTSBURGH, PENNSYLVANIA

Contents

Introduction
Chapter 1

An appreciation for the Old Testament is a basic aspect of our Christian faith. The Old Testament is significant because its subject matter is divine revelation and it brings into focus the indisputable reality of God's action in the life and history of the Hebrew people. Through knowledge of this history we come to understand the context for the life of Jesus, the Christ. The background for understanding the person of Jesus as well as his message is found in the Old Testament stories and history.

STUDYING THE STORIES OF THE OLD TESTAMENT

Why should Christians pay so much attention to the Old Testament? When Christians study the Sermon on the Mount seriously, they will remember Jesus saying that he did not come to create a new law but rather to rejuvenate, fulfill, and humanize the existing one, on God's terms. It must be remembered, too, that Christ was a Jew, and if for no other reason than the intellectual integrity of ferreting out the background of Jesus, a Christian should study the Old Testament documents carefully.

Many scholars have studied the Old Testament with their own favorite tools and from their own respective disciplines. Much of the important writing has come from German biblical scholarship of the last three centuries. For example, J. G. Eichorn in the eighteenth century seems to have been the first to study the Bible from a "scientific" or research perspective. He made a careful study of three main subjects:

- the origin of the canon—how the books of the Bible came to be accepted as the official Christian record that they are;
- the history of the text;

• the origins of the different books, knowledge about the sources. From this research and method of study, Julius Wellhausen went further to identify what he felt were four interwoven authors' accounts of the Pentateuch (the first five books of the Old Testament).

Later, another German scholar, Hermann Gunkel, contended that the key to the understanding of the Old Testament was an analysis of its literary form. In other words, in the way that an art critic can tell that two paintings are probably from different centuries and schools (ethnic or geographic traditions), he felt that parts of the Old Testament could be analyzed and labeled from different times in Judaic history and different customs of the extended families of tribes and small nations.

Archaeologists from all parts of the world have found artifacts of tools and papyrus writings which "flesh out" the Old Testament daily living and transitions from era to era.

In addition to the scientific research theories, the linguistic analyses, and the archaeological re-creations of probable life-styles, anthropologists have emphasized the religion of the Old Testament as a part of all human history. In this sense what the Old Testament describes is seen in the broad light of universal human experience. Sociologists have added their contribution by studying religion as a group happening, not an individual spiritual response. Also historians have analyzed the interaction of religious institutions with political, economic, and other cultural forms.

In recent years there has been a new interest in the body of writings in the Old Testament called "wisdom literature" (Job, Proverbs, Ecclesiastes, and Song of Solomon). These writings are interesting, too, for a psychologist or a literary scholar. Written in poetic form, wisdom literature appears to be the apex of understanding how generations of families reflected upon their internal struggles toward right relationship within themselves, with each other, and with God. Finally, contemporary Christian theologians show renewed interest in the Old Testament as a recital of the acts of God in history. This concern is central to Old Testament study for the lay person. It is no longer sufficient to ask, "What are the facts, ideas, and stories of the Old Testament?" but "What is the theological significance which this assembled history reveals about God, people, and salvation?"

To many lay people the approaches of disciplines such as anthropology, sociology, or the use of the scientific method in research of the Bible seem to violate a sense of sacred inspiration of Scripture. However, this need not be so. There can be an honestly integral relationship between historical and scientific methods of criticism and theological interpretation. The Old Testament is the recital of God's acts in history. Underlying "The Book" is God's revelation of himself, not only in the experience of the Hebrew people, but also in the interpretation of the writers.

The late G. Ernest Wright, professor of Old Testament Studies at Harvard Divinity School, in his perceptive chapter "Theology as Recital," makes it clear that the starting point for biblical faith is not the development of religious ideas, nor is it a systematic cross section of such ideas under the heading of a dogmatic theology. He argues that biblical theology is first and foremost a theology of "recital" in which biblical people confess their faith by recalling and then celebrating the formative events of their history as the redemptive handiwork of God. Therefore, Wright concluded that the key elements in the Old Testament theology are: (1) the peculiar attention given to history and to historical tradition as the primary sphere in which God makes himself known, (2) the election of a special people through whom God mediates himself, and (3) the confirmation and clarification of this election and its implications in the covenant ceremony at Sinai. Wright sets a meaningful focus, seeing the Old Testament as the "acts of God" in the experience of the Hebrew people. His emphasis upon the Old Testament as the recital of God's revelation to Israel places in perspective the role of scientific and dogmatic approaches to the study of the Old Testament.[1]

THREE KEYS: EXPERIENCE, UNDERSTANDING, AND CROSSING POINT

This review of the recent developments in Old Testament studies has attempted to point out the trends in the study of the Old Testament. However, if we are to understand the Old Testament as relating the experiences of faith of the Hebrew people, we must examine how the faith of God's people functioned in great pivotal periods and crises. It was out of this interaction between God's acts of revelation and Israel's experiences that the Old Testament emerged.

The following questions will serve as a guide to begin our examination of these pivotal periods:

1. What were the *experiences* of Israel which formed the basis of the Old Testament faith?
2. What was the Hebrew *understanding* of these experiences?
3. What is the *crossing point* between the Hebrews' experience and understanding and our life today?

The method of the author will be to present the experience of the Hebrews as it is recorded in the Scripture. In the books under discussion there is a wide variety of literary materials. These will be noted in connection with the particular books under discussion. The author will hold to a minimum the problems of literary criticism except when determination of the best alternative readings are essential for an understanding of the text. For instance, a passage from Deuteronomy can serve as a concise example of the core of Israel's faith:

> "And you shall make response before the Lord your God, 'A wandering Aramean was my father; and he went down into Egypt and sojourned there, few in number; and there he became a nation, great, mighty, and populous. And the Egyptians treated us harshly, and afflicted us, and laid upon us hard bondage. Then we cried to the Lord the God of our fathers, and the Lord heard our voice, and saw our affliction, our toil, and our oppression; and the Lord brought us out of Egypt with a mighty hand and with an outstretched arm, with great terror, with signs and wonders; and he brought us into this place and gave us this land, a land flowing with milk and honey. And behold, now I bring the first of the fruit of the ground, which thou, O Lord, hast given me.' And you shall set it down before the Lord your God, and worship before the Lord your God; and you shall rejoice in all the good which the Lord your God has given to you and to your house, you, and the Levite, and the sojourner who is among you" (Deuteronomy 26:5-11).

This passage contains the significant aspects of the Hebrew religious experience:

1. The experience of encountering God.
2. The experience in dire circumstances.
3. The experiences of a community. The occasion for this Hebrew

affirmation of faith was the offering of the firstfruits to God.

The point of focus is God; the offering is a celebration of God's acts and deeds in their history: "And you shall make your response before your God" (v. 5). The writer emphasizes the experience of God in Israel's life—God is depicted as an active and powerful redeemer: "The Lord heard our voice . . . the Lord brought us out of Egypt . . . he brought us into this place . . ." (vv. 7-9). The Hebrew faith began as the Hebrew people experienced God. They knew that he had manifested himself mightily to them!

This passage reflects the biblical writer's belief that the experience of God had come in dire circumstances. The Hebrews had experienced many things in Egypt. The children of Jacob (Israel) began with a few people. They became a great nation. They were treated harshly and suffered in bondage. They experienced toil and oppression. The Hebrews' existence in Egypt was hard and difficult, but God released them from great terrors with "signs and wonders."

Their experience was shared by the total community. ". . . the Egyptians treated *us* harshly, and afflicted *us,* and laid upon *us* hard bondage" (v. 6). However, in these oppressions they experienced a unity in their suffering. "Then *we* cried to the Lord" (v. 7). Their collective suffering forged them into a unit. Their total consciousness experienced God and each other, even in dire circumstances.

Also this text expresses the writer's religious interpretation of all of these aspects of the Hebrews' experience. The Hebrews saw the Egyptian bondage and subsequent release as evidence of God's care and concern. The biblical writer saw their total experience as an act of God: "And the Lord brought us out of Egypt with a mighty hand and an outstretched arm, with great terror, with signs and wonders" (v. 8).

What is the crossing point between this ancient creedal recital and the church's faith? First, this Old Testament creed emphasizes the sovereignty of God. In a similar fashion the Apostles' Creed, recited in many churches today, begins with the affirmation of God's sovereignty: "I believe in God, the Father Almighty. . . ." Christian faith begins with the affirmation that God is Lord of the universe.

Secondly, this creedal statement affirms God's action in history. The Hebrews saw God's action in the promise of the patriarchs, their deliverance from Egypt, the leadership in the wilderness, their settlement in the land, and God's revelation at Sinai. Although these events are evidences of God's revelation, the Christian's affirmation of God's act in history is primarily through the incarnation of Jesus Christ. The Apostles' Creed states this poignantly:

> and in Jesus Christ, His only Son our Lord; who was conceived by the Holy Ghost, born of the Virgin Mary, suffered under Pontius Pilate, was crucified, dead, and buried; He descended into hell; the third day He rose from the dead; He ascended into heaven, and sitteth at the right hand of God the Father Almighty; from thence He shall come to judge the quick and the dead. . . .

Finally, the context of this confession of faith speaks of the responsibility of the individual to respond. The worshipers in Old Testament times were required to present an offering of firstfruits as a symbol of their response to God. We also are called upon to respond to God's acts of love. Faith is responding in love to God's outpouring of himself in Jesus, the Christ. Like the ancient Hebrew worshiper, we can praise God in thanksgiving and not only offer our firstfruits but also offer ourselves to him. The belief in the sovereignty of God and his action in history is the key crossing point between Hebrew faith and ours. Let us examine more closely some of the other crossing points between Hebrew faith and ours.

QUESTIONS FOR FURTHER CONSIDERATION

• If we believe in the sovereignty of God and that we have a responsibility to respond, how do we as Christians respond to the injustices around us?

• Does God *still* function in history on the side of the oppressed? Does God function as a God of justice in history? What specific evidences do you have for your answers to these questions?

• Will God take away the blessing from the nation that acts in self-interest and greed? Are we guilty of self-interest and greed as we allow children to attend poor quality schools; when we fail to provide adequate financial support for mental institutions?

The Hebrew Thoughts About Creation

Chapter 2

Recently I visited a friend in western Pennsylvania. The golden hues of autumn had begun to tint the foliage of the trees. As I walked along the road with my friend, we both were overawed by the beauty of such heavenly splendor. We could appreciate the experience that led the Hebrew writer to exclaim, "In the beginning God. . . ." The purpose of this chapter is to study the two biblical accounts of God as Creator. The focus of the first account (Genesis 1:1–2:4) is the praising of God as Creator. The focus of the second account (Genesis 2:46–3:24) is humankind's innocence and disobedience. Each of these accounts will be examined in the light of the three keys: experience, understanding, and crossing point.

GOD IS PRAISED AS CREATOR (Genesis 1:1–2:4a)
The Experience

One of the significant results of modern biblical scholarship has been its location of the times or period out of which the basic documents emerged. It is generally agreed that Genesis 1:1–2:4a was a document which emerged during the sixth century B.C. The experience out of which this document emerged was the exilic period when the Hebrews were away from their homes, away from their loved ones, and in bondage. We will treat this period more exhaustively in a later chapter. It is sufficient here to understand that the beautiful and psalmatic description of God as Creator in Genesis was written during a period in which the Israelite state had collapsed and the people were in exile. It was from among a deported people that the affirmation was made: "In the beginning God . . ." (Genesis 1:1).

Their experience was characterized by the loss of three things which were very important in their lives. They had lost their nation. The Northern Kingdom fell in 722 B.C. and the Southern Kingdom followed in 597 B.C. and 586 B.C. The glory and grandeur of the Davidic and Solomonic period were replaced by existence in colonies under different foreign kings. Their mood is aptly described in Psalm 137:1-3:

> By the waters of Babylon, there we sat down and
>   wept, when we remembered Zion.
> On the willows there we hung up our lyres.
> For there our captors required of us songs,
>   and our tormentors, mirth, saying,
>   "Sing us one of the songs of Zion!"

They had lost their temple. It was destroyed by armies of the Babylonians. The despair caused by this is expressed in Psalm 74:1-10:

O God, why dost thou cast us off for ever?
Why does thy anger smoke against the sheep of thy pasture?
Remember thy congregation, which thou hast gotten of old,
    which thou has redeemed to be the tribe of thy heritage!
    Remember Mount Zion, where thou hast dwelt.
Direct thy steps to the perpetual ruins;
    the enemy has destroyed everything in the sanctuary!

Thy foes have roared in the midst of thy holy place;
    they set up their own signs for signs.
At the upper entrance they hacked the wooden trellis with axes.
And then all its carved wood they broke down with hatchets and
    hammers.
They set thy sanctuary on fire;
    to the ground they desecrated the dwelling place of thy name.
They said to themselves, "We will utterly subdue them";
    they burned all the meeting places of God in the land.

We do not see our signs;
    there is no longer any prophet,
    and there is none among us who knows how long.

How long, O God, is the foe to scoff?
    Is the enemy to revile thy name forever?

Jerusalem, which had been the center of their worship, had been completely destroyed. The central place in their religious life was ruined during the siege by the Babylonian armies from 597–586 B.C. Jerusalem was now a desolate city.

They had lost their leaders. All of the upper-class families were deported to a foreign land, and they were treated as less than human. Their leaders were constantly reminded of the superiority of the Babylonian civilization and of the Babylonian God Marduk. This period will be discussed in more detail in chapter 9.

The Understanding

However, the Hebrew writers did not understand their experience in a way that one would expect. One would suspect that a deported and exiled people would have denied their faith and turned their backs on God. On the contrary, from among the exiles in Babylon there emerged the creation story which celebrated God as the Creator. This was the experience upon which they reflected. Thus we ask: "How did these writers understand this experience?" In the midst of all their hardship and struggles they felt that God was with them. Although their burdens were hard, they believed that his presence was sufficient for their every need.

Their understanding of their experience is expressed in the words of the writers of the creation story in Genesis 1. God is Creator! God is Lord!

The Hebrews felt strongly the loss of their nation. They longed for Jerusalem:

> If I forget you, O Jerusalem,
>   let my right hand wither!
> Let my tongue cleave to the roof of my mouth,
>   if I do not remember you,
> if I do not set Jerusalem
>   above my highest joy!
>
> —Psalm 137:5f.

Nevertheless, they understood that the loss of the land was in no way evidence that God was not with them. On the contrary, they came to the realization that nationhood was not physical but spiritual. The tie which bound them together was that they were sons and daughters of a powerful Creator who had created light out of darkness, something out of nothing.

They also felt the need to examine the meaning of the loss of their temple. The temple was very important in the life of the Hebrews. Over and over again they praised God for the temple. Solomon's prayer of dedication reflects this sense of praise (2 Chronicles 6:1-11).

In spite of this catastrophe (the loss of their temple), they believed that God was beyond the temple. The Exile forced them to understand that the true object of worship was not the temple but the God who made the earth, the sky, and the seas. They anticipated the words of Jesus when he spoke to the woman at the well in Samaria: "God is spirit, and those who worship him must worship in spirit and truth" (John 4:24). They understood the destruction of the temple to mean God's wrath on their sins and his challenge to them to understand him as he really was, the Creator of all the ends of the earth. Also they had to understand the meaning of the deportation of their leaders as told by the chronicler: "He took into exile in Babylon those who had escaped from the sword, and they became servants to him and to his sons until the establishment of the kingdom of Persia" (2 Chronicles 36:20). This was seen in fulfillment of the prophecy of Jeremiah: "To fulfil the word of the Lord by the mouth of Jeremiah, until the land had enjoyed its sabbaths. All the days that it lay desolate it kept sabbath, to fulfil seventy years" (2 Chronicles 36:21). The spirit that undergirds the writing of the first creation story is joy and gladness. This mood was due to their recognition that dependence was not upon earthly leaders who were sons of Adam, but upon the God who called forth order out of chaos. Let us look at this account in more detail.

The purpose of the biblical authors of the first three chapters of Genesis is not to give a scientific study of creation; nor are they attempting to treat the idea of God in a philosophical way. Clearly the writers are presenting their understanding of the acts of God as "Creator." It was to his creative acts that the Hebrews responded.

As we study these chapters of Genesis, we are aware that although these are not eyewitness accounts, they were a part of Hebrew tradition a long time before they were written in the form in which we have them. At least four stages are suggested by the accounts. First, there was the period of oral transmission in which the inspired poet began to sing about the joys of creation. The second period was the writing down of the older account in Genesis, chapters 2 and 3, with the emphasis upon innocence, sin, judgment, and forgiveness. This was followed by the third stage when the writers living in exile put into writing the oral accounts from the perspective of God's power and authority. The final stage was the collation of all of the basic accounts into one unit underlying this total process with the faith in God as Creator of all things created.

One is impressed by the simplicity and concreteness of the writers of the creation accounts. They do not use abstract ideas as the basis of their story of the creation. The content of their understanding rests upon direct observation. They were aware that existence was the result of an intentional act of God. They believed that all of the things which they encountered daily were somehow related to their Creator.

Let us look at the basic elements in the Genesis accounts which grew out of their experiences. "The earth was without form and void" (1:2). At the very beginning the Hebrews observed that there was order in the universe. This became for them a significant aspect of creation. They knew that morning followed evening, that the seasons followed a rhythmic pattern, that nature was not arbitrary or capricious but responded to a definite law. Therefore they reasoned that order emerged out of chaos since they felt that this order did not happen accidentally. The experience of order gave them an understanding that God was the Creator who brought order out of chaos.

"And God said 'Let there be light'" (1:3). The Hebrews noticed the light of the sun. They were reminded daily of the contrast between darkness and light. They could also see that order and light were related. The existence of light helped them to observe the reality of order. In their daily living light was crucial. Waking, walking, and working were made possible by light. The sun gave nourishing food. It controlled their planting and harvesting. Light provided the framework for their style of work, their times of beginning and ending. It was also integral to their social relationships. Days, months, and years were regulated by the cycles of the sun. These many experiences related to the light of the sun helped develop their understanding of God as the Creator of light.

"And God said 'Let the waters under the heavens . . .'" (1:9-10).

Then the Hebrews saw the world divided into firmament (sky) and waters above and below it. The imagery of a three-part universe and the separation of earth (land) and seas (water) below the heavens suggested living space for the natural categories of living things they observed. God's abode was heaven although he came to the earth many times and in many forms. The "waters" under the heavens eventually provided dry land and sea, places for the habitation of humans who shared it with the birds, fish, and animals.

However primitive this world picture, we must not overlook the significant point that the Hebrew writers made. They had experienced a place to be somebody, some place in which to live and act. This awareness of a definite place or home for the human family underlies the inclusion of the firmament as a part of the creation story. In addition, the Hebrew writers realized that there were other elements in the created universe which they experienced, such as the sea, vegetation, sun, moon, and the stars. They included these elements in their accounts. They understood that these were all gifts from God.

"And God said, 'Let the waters . . . earth'" (1:20-22). Also the Hebrews' experience taught them that there were other "living things" in the world: birds, fishes, and sea creatures. These "living things" were a part of their everyday life. Therefore, these creatures were included in the total recognition of the things made and given by God.

It is significant that all of the elements of the Hebrew creation grew out of things they saw and did every day. The elements described in their creation stories were so obvious that it may seem trivial to list them. However, it is in this ordinariness, this commonness, that we see the critical significance of their reflective genius. The Hebrews looked at their world of experience and, upon reflection, interpreted these as evidence of the total creation by God. The Genesis writers took more time to describe the creation of humans than the rest of the universe. They believed that people were special. This view of humankind is expressed dramatically in the following verse which begins with the special creation of human beings: "And God said, 'Let us make [human creatures] in our own image . . .'" (1:26ff.).

The Hebrew author described the characteristics of humankind in several ways. Humankind was separate from the rest of creation—

special! God's creation on the sixth day was seen not only as the completion of creation but also as a climax of the creative drama. Men and women existed sexually in harmonious relationship to one another! "Male and female he created them." They were not viewed as opponents. Both were part of the inherent unity of humankind. Humankind shared responsibility to maintain the world. Humankind had a special vocation, a unique calling to share with God in the lordship over the universe. They were given noble work. Human beings were a part of the total process of creation. They were in many ways a part of nature, and yet different from nature. Humans had to abide by the same laws of nature—birth and death, growth and decay—as all other parts of the creation. Men and women were also called upon to reproduce themselves and care for one another in love.

Finally the writers observed that humankind needed a time for rest. "So God blessed the seventh day and hallowed it, because on it God rested from all his work which he had done in creation" (Genesis 2:3). Work was important but rest was also a necessity. Thus, the final experience that the Hebrew included within the creation drama was rest (sleep, relaxation, reflection). He saw this as an important part of individual and community experience; so it was attributed to imitation of a divine act. The Creator rests from his work on the seventh day, and this becomes the sanction of the Jewish sabbath rest.

We have presented what has been traditionlly referred to as the eight works of creation: creation of light (Genesis 1:3-5); creation of the firmament (Genesis 1:6-8); creation of dry land and sea (Genesis 1:9-10); creation of plants (Genesis 1:11-13); creation of the heavenly luminaries (Genesis 1:14-19); creation of sea animals and winged animals (Genesis 1:20-23); creation of land animals (Genesis 1:24-25); and creation of humankind (Genesis 1:26-31).

We can summarize this section by saying that the Hebrew writers used their common daily experiences as the context and content of their accounts of creation. They presented their story of creation from a divine perspective. God was revealed in the totality of their experiences.

Apart from the facts of the creation accounts, it is important to note that in the first three chapters of Genesis there are two accounts written by two different authors. In the first account the author celebrates the activity of God as Creator through his word. The whole account could be summarized in the following sentence: "God created an orderly world out of chaos and assigned people a preeminent place." Instead, the poet says, "In the beginning God created the heavens and the earth." Some writers suggest, "When God began to create. . . ." The intent is very clear. God's activity as Creator is the point of focus. Only He brings order out of chaos. God's lordship is also expressed in the method of creation. He created by his word: "And God said, 'Let there be light'; and there was light." Creation by God's word is celebrated in Psalm 33:6-9:

> By the word of the Lord the heavens were made,
>   and all their host by the breath of his mouth.
> He gathered the waters of the sea as in a bottle;
>   he put the deeps in storehouses.
> Let all the earth fear the Lord,
>   let all the inhabitants of the world stand in awe of him!
> For he spoke, and it came to be;
>   he commanded, and it stood forth.

The experience of the exile enabled the Hebrews to understand the meaning of God as Creator. Although weak and powerless, the understanding that the Almighty God was Creator of the world gave them a new perspective of their situation.

The Crossing Point

As we reflect upon the crossing point between the Hebrew understanding of creation from the exilic experience and our Christian faith today, we are reminded of a recent creed that comes to us from the United Church of Christ. This creed states:

We believe in God, the Eternal Spirit, Father of our Lord Jesus Christ and our Father, and to his deeds we testify:
    He calls the world into being, creates man in his own image and sets before him the ways of life and death.

This is a dynamic message for us in our time of weakness and powerlessness.

The story is told of a young student who denied the reality of God. To publicize his belief, he wrote above his bed the sign "GOD IS

NOWHERE." One night when he returned home in a mood of despondency and dejection, as he entered the room and looked at the sign, instead of reading "GOD IS NOWHERE," the words seemed to read "GOD IS NOW HERE!" This is what the Hebrew writers found in the midst of the Exile! This is our experience.

"GOD IS NOW HERE!" The Apostles' Creed also affirms "the Maker of heaven and earth." The creation story dramatizes this reality. However prescientific their world view, the writers were inspired by God. They believed that the world was made by the God who was with them in the Exile.

This is the legacy for us who read these stories. They point beyond the world to God, the Creator—God who is the Almighty—who demonstrates his power by the creation of the world. The phrases "Let there be" and "It was so" indicate God's authority.

These two points, God's reality and his authority, speak to the key issues in the world today. The biblical writers help us to understand the way the many Hebrews during the Exile understood the problem of faith. God was the Almighty—the Maker of heaven and earth. This is the crossing point—this is where our faith intersects the Hebrew faith today!

Several years ago the late Dean Samuel Miller of Harvard Divinity School spoke to the opening convocation of the school on the "Sacrament of Failure." His thesis was that failure can become demonic—it can destroy; but it can also become therapeutic—it can save. From the circle of religious leaders from whom we get the creation story in Genesis 1:1–2:46, failure was a sacrament. From the ash heap of the Exile the writers looked up and proclaimed: "In the beginning God. . . . " This is also our faith!

HUMANKIND'S INNOCENCE AND DISOBEDIENCE
(Genesis 2:4b–3:24)
The Experience

The experience out of which the second creation account comes is quite different. This document is dated during the reigns of David and Solomon in the tenth and ninth centuries B.C. In contrast to the time of the Exile, this period was characterized by prosperity and success in which they celebrated the glory of their land, their temple, and their leaders. We will be treating this period in more detail in our chapter on the founding and the development of the monarchy. We mention this period at this point to focus upon the fact that the temptations which the people faced in this period were not despair and despondency, but self-sufficiency and arrogance! It was out of this experience that the Hebrew writer presents the account of humankind's tragic plight. The fact that his people were succumbing to apathy and false security led the author to remind his readers of the true estate of humankind, one of sinfulness and rebellion against God. In spite of the outward prosperity and national success, the Hebrews flirted with the gods of the neighboring tribes and often forgot God.

The writer interprets the significance of this period for his readers. He recapitulates the traditional narratives in the form of a forceful drama of the true relationship between humanity and God. God is the Creator! Humankind is expected to live in harmony with God.

The Understanding

The Creation

The second account of the creation stories begins with the creation of humankind and ends with "the fall" (Genesis 2:4b–3:24). The basic thrust of this story is the loss of innocence on the part of all human beings and the subsequent expulsion of Adam and Eve from the Garden of Eden. There are several points of contrast between chapters 1 and 2:

In *chapter 1* the author gives a precise, schematic presentation of the creation.

In *chapter 2* the author assumes the creation has already taken place.

In *chapter 1* the first condition of the world is described as "without form and void" and completely dark (Genesis 1:2). On the contrary, *chapter 2* sees the condition of the world as an arid, waterless waste (Genesis 2:5f.).

In *chapter 1* the order of created works is presented as light, firmament, earth, vegetation, sun, moon, stars, birds, animals, man, whereas *chapter 2* presents the following order: man, trees, animals, and woman.

However, the two accounts agree in supplementary features, such as the garden of the miraculous trees and human position in the world.

Theologically, there are at least two noteworthy points of contrast which we find in this second account. First, the experience of God is that of one who comes among his people. Unlike the author of Genesis 1 who lifts God high above humankind "over and above his creation," the author of Genesis 2 and 3 presents God in everyday language by saying that God walks in his garden in the cool of the day (Genesis 3:8) and God is concerned for the welfare of his creatures (Genesis 2:18ff.). He conducts an examination to confront man and woman with their sin. This radical contrast in the understanding of God is significant in that the emphasis in Genesis 2 and 3 is upon God who becomes involved in what he has created. Theologically, this understanding of God is at the heart of the New Testament meaning of incarnation. In the New Testament God comes in Jesus Christ as Immanuel—"God with us."

A second point worth noting is the understanding of human beings which underlies this story. In Genesis 1 it was sufficient for the writer to describe the creation of humankind in glowing terms. In contrast, the writer of the second account depicts humankind in terms of created innocence and subsequent fall. The dominant character of the drama is still God. But the focus is here upon humankind, who, with such glowing possibilities, disobeyed God and had to be expelled from the garden. We will look closely at this drama.

The author presents the creation of the man: "Then the Lord God formed man of dust from the ground, and breathed into his nostrils the breath of life; and man became a living being" (Genesis 2:7). He then makes the reader aware of the barrenness of the earth; this was the original destiny of humankind. It is clear that this description is the picture of the land before flora and fauna. Two more things were absent—rain and cultivation. Both would be supplied by God. The rest of the story tells how God made the world capable of cultivation.

The author uses the imagery of the potter to illustrate his story. The Hebrew word is translated *mold*. In verse 7 one finds the classic description of the Old Testament understanding of the nature of human life. The key Hebrew word is *nephesh*—breath. The point that the author is making is that humankind received vitality directly from God. The fact that they thought that God gave life by breathing into man's own nostrils is a mark of dignity. It is the same idea of the image of God which we found in the account of Genesis 1:26.

The author continues the human creation story with an idyllic picture of the Garden of Eden:

> And the Lord God planted a garden in Eden, in the east; and there he put the man whom he had formed. And out of the ground the Lord God made to grow every tree that is pleasant to the sight and good for food, the tree of life also in the midst of the garden, and the tree of the knowledge of good and evil.

> A river flowed out of Eden to water the garden, and there it divided and became four rivers. The name of the first is Pishon; it is the one which flows around the whole land of Havilah, where there is gold; and the gold of that land is good; bdellium and onyx stone are there. The name of the second river is Gihon; it is the one which flows around the whole land of Cush. And the name of the third river is Tigris, which flows east of Assyria. And the fourth river is the Euphrates (Genesis 2:8-14).

A similar idea of a divine garden is also found in Genesis 13:10 and Ezekiel 28:13. Although the phrase "Garden of Eden" is indicated in the passage as a geographical place, the original phrase here is normally translated a "garden of delight." In this garden there were many trees; among them was the tree of life which was believed to bestow eternal life (Genesis 3:22) and the tree of knowledge of good and evil which was thought to confer wisdom. There were also four rivers which flowed out of the garden to the four corners of the known world.

This description of the idyllic garden includes two key concluding comments. On the one hand, people were given responsibility for the upkeep of the garden: "to till it and keep it." On the other hand, they were given permission to eat of all the trees in the garden except the tree of knowledge about good and evil. This last verse suggests God's lordship and human obedience to him.

In the next section the author treats the creation of animals and then of women. The author speaks of Adam's need for a companion suitable for him. After noting the creation of the animals and the naming of them, which is interpreted as man's lordship, the author depicts the creation of woman. The use of Adam's rib suggests the essential affinity between men and women. In this story the sexual attraction between man and woman is also affirmed.

All of the material presented above is a reflection upon the experience of the Hebrew writers in their relationship to God, each other, and nature. These accounts show that the Hebrews believed that creation in all of its glory and grandeur is a work of God. Genesis 2 ends with a note of great expectation. God has given the prototypical man and woman a noble creation (out of his own breath), a beautiful garden (the Garden of Eden), and the earth populated with vegetation and animals. What will people do with this blessed state? In Genesis 3 we find the answer. Humankind disobeys God and is expelled from the Garden of Eden.

The Disobedience

The story of humankind's fall is an integral part of the author's account of the creation. An examination of the vocabulary style, imagery, and movement reveals that the writer of the story of the creation of man and woman (Genesis 2:4b-25) is the same person who wrote the account of the fall (Genesis 3:1-24). The biblical author's conviction is that humankind, which was created in innocence, disobeyed God and is now in a condition of alienation from him.

The account begins with a discussion of the serpent (Genesis 3:1-3), "a beast of the field." Although the serpent was presented as a creature of God, it was also used here to symbolize hostility to God and the distortion of truth. The conversation began between Eve and the serpent and continued as the serpent denied the inevitability of punishment and suggested likeness to God as a real alternative (Genesis 3:4-5). The woman was tempted, and she yielded. Then she tempted her husband (v. 6). They then became aware of their nakedness and hid from God. This is the manifestation of their sin (v. 7).

The fellowship in the Garden of Eden was disrupted (Genesis 3:8-13). The garden which was a "place of delight" became a place of fear and alienation: ". . . and I was afraid" (v. 10). The garden became a scene of charges and countercharges.

Following the eating of the fruit, the man made an implicit accusation against God: "The woman you gave me for a companion, she gave me fruit from the tree and I ate it" (Genesis 3:12, NEB).

When God asked the woman about her role, she accused the serpent: "The serpent tricked me, and I ate" (Genesis 3:14a, NEB). These accusations were due to the fact that their sin had been discovered by God.

The next two sections of this chapter (Genesis 3) treat the curse (Genesis 3:14-19) and the expulsion from Eden (Genesis 3:20-24). They complete the drama of humankind's fall and the consequences therewith. Let us look at the curse. In the following passage all three parties are given specific punishments:

The serpent (Genesis 3:14-15):

> The Lord God said to the serpent,
> "Because you have done this,
>   cursed are you above all cattle,
>   and above all wild animals;
>   upon your belly you shall go,
>   and dust you shall eat
>   all the days of your life.
>   I will put enmity between you and the woman,
>   and between your seed and her seed;
>   he shall bruise your head,
>   and you shall bruise his heel."

The woman (Genesis 3:16):

> To the woman he said,
> "I will greatly multiply your pain in childbearing;
>   in pain you shall bring forth children,
> yet your desire shall be for your husband,
>   and he shall rule over you."

The man (Genesis 3:17-19):

> And to Adam he said,
> "Because you have listened to the voice of your wife,
>   and have eaten of the tree
> of which I commanded you,
>   'You shall not eat of it,'
> cursed is the ground because of you;
>   in toil you shall eat of it all the days of your life;

thorns and thistles it shall bring forth to you;
    and you shall eat the plants of the field.
In the sweat of your face
    you shall eat bread
till you return to the ground,
    for out of it you were taken;
you are dust,   .
    and to dust you shall return."

The curse of the serpent is an attempt to explain the reason why serpents have no legs—this implies that previously they did walk. The second aspect of the curse, "I will put enmity between you and the woman" (v. 15), is unclear at some points.

Despite the many interpretations, this verse suggests the enmity established between the serpent and the human race, and the feud between them is the evidence of the serpent's crawling on the ground and humans' walking upright.

The next curse is pronounced upon the woman (v. 16). The first part of the verse speaks of the origin of pain suffered by woman in childbirth. The pangs of childbirth are often used illustratively for human suffering (Isaiah 21:3; 13:8; part of the Maccabbees 4:9; Psalm 48:6). The second part of the verse is subject to many interpretations. Whether one translates this as the sexual desire of the woman or her desire to bear children, the text reflects the author's reference to dependence upon her husband. One must hasten to add that the author is not describing an ideal situation but rather a situation that is the result of humankind's sin. Thus, although some might interpret from this passage the subordination of woman by man, one should note that this is a consequence of man's deviation from God's order of equality which was established by God before the fall.

Next the curse is addressed to man (vv. 17-19). Here "the man" is punished by being prohibited from eating from the tree. His evil also caused the ground to be cursed. Thus, man's relationship with God and man's relationship with nature are corrupted. Therefore, instead of humankind enjoying all kinds of fruit in the garden for food, he now tills the earth which responds with nothing but thorns and briars. If he is to eat, it must be through the "sweat of the brow." Although the fact of death is mentioned, the author does not say whether humans would have actually lived forever if they had not yielded to temptation. His only point in this passage is that death is inescapable.

Finally the author concludes this drama of human pilgrimage from created innocence to expulsion from the garden. After the naming of Eve "mother of the living," brief reference is made to the clothing of Adam and Eve. The final comment refers to their expulsion from Eden.

Our review of the creation stories in Genesis 1–3 has been made in order for us to deal with the texts themselves. What insights do we gain from this view of creation and the fall? What is the crossing point?

The Crossing Point

Paul Ricoeur, contemporary French theologian, pinpoints the insight we gain from biblical writers when he states that this story ". . . is the fruit of the prophetic accusation directed against man; the same theology that makes God innocent accuses man."[1] The basic thrust of the creation account in Genesis 2 and 3 is a call for human repentance. This is the decision this story seeks to evoke. Humankind has missed the mark, but God is still Creator and still loves the creation. The biblical writer paints this picture of human tragedy in moving strokes of despair but also challenges us with humankind's originally marvelous possibilities in partnership with God.

Further, as we seek to determine the crossing point between the creation story in Genesis 2 and 3, it becomes obvious that the Hebrew view of humankind expresses the same view that we as Christians hold—God created humankind in innocence and humankind sinned and therefore came under the judgment of God. Nevertheless, through grace we can be restored to be the persons that God intended when he created us.

The Hebrew belief in humankind's innocence stresses the goodness of God's creation. Christian scholars have also insisted that humankind was originally created good. The point here is that disobedience led to this change in relationship with God. Therefore, like the Hebrew writers we affirm belief in the reality of human sin. There is no attempt to blame God for sin. It is rooted in humankind's rejection of the authority of God. No matter how we interpret the fall, we agree with the Hebrew writers that sin is rooted in the conscience of created beings.

God's holiness and righteousness require that he call sin into accountability. Thus, judgment comes as a result of human rejection of divine authority. Judgment is God's requiring the sinner to look responsibly at sin. Judgment also is an opportunity for repentance.

But the Christian's appropriation of the Hebrew's concept of innocence, sin, and judgment focuses more sharply upon grace than did the Old Testament writers. The Old Testament writers' strong sense of retribution reduced the possibility of unmerited favor of God. The unmerited favor of God is one of the strongest aspects of the Christian faith. Although we sin, we can accept grace. The meaning of grace is aptly illustrated in the following story:

> ... but Jesus went to the Mount of Olives. Early in the morning he came again to the temple; all the people came to him, and he sat down and taught them. The scribes and the Pharisees brought a woman who had been caught in adultery, and placing her in the midst they said to him, "Teacher, this woman has been caught in the act of adultery. Now in the law Moses commanded us to stone such. What do you say about her?" This they said to test him, that they might have some charge to bring against him. Jesus bent down and wrote with his finger on the ground. And as they continued to ask him, he stood up and said to them, "Let him who is without sin among you be the first to throw a stone at her." And once more he bent down and wrote with his finger on the ground. But when they heard it, they went away, one by one, beginning with the eldest, and Jesus was left alone with the woman standing before him. Jesus looked up and said to her, "Woman, where are they? Has no one condemned you?" She said, "No one, Lord." And Jesus said, "Neither do I condemn you; go, and do not sin again" (John 7:53–8:11).

(The RSV places this story in a footnote since it is omitted from several of the old manuscripts. Nevertheless, this story is illustrative of Jesus' treatment of the sinner. This episode illustrates the Christian view of forgiveness.)

James Gordon Gilkey, writing in a book several years ago entitled *The Problem of Following Jesus,* has suggested that Jesus articulated two basic truths: that at the heart of life there is a God who loves all human beings so dearly that each of us can trust himself or herself to that God; that every human being, no matter how small, weak, or helpless, is a child of God. This is the legacy of the concept of God which we find in the second creation account. This is the crossing point. The God who created humankind in innocence is also the God that we can trust to forgive us, even though we have sinned. Even in our sinfulness we are his children.

In contrition the Christian affirms in Jesus Christ that God forgives our sins, or, as the Apostles' Creed confesses, "I believe in . . . the forgiveness of sins."

QUESTIONS FOR FURTHER CONSIDERATION

- How far are human beings alone the cause of sin, and how much is the necessity of sin inherent in creation?
- Do you agree that sin is the desire for knowledge, to no longer be dependent, childlike, before God? Why or why not?
- Does the command to develop fully in humanity imply the responsibility of knowledge, of using the created brain?
- At what point does the necessity for God's forgiveness enter if there is to be a nonguilty relationship between Creator and creature?
- Does humankind's misuse of natural resources in terms of polluting the air and water show evidence of human sin? If so, what acts of repentance are required?

The Patriarchs:
The Pioneers of Faith

Chapter 3

The writer of the Epistle to the Hebrews gives us a perspective for assessing the role of the patriarchs in the formation of Hebrew faith. The patriarchs are presented as inspired leaders who demonstrated the meaning of faith.

> By faith Abraham obeyed the call to go out to a land destined for himself and his heirs, and left home without knowing where he was to go. By faith he settled as an alien in the land promised him, living in tents, as did Isaac and Jacob, who were heirs to the same promise. For he was looking forward to the city with firm foundations, whose architect and builder is God (Hebrews 11:8-10, NEB).

This glowing tribute from the early church sees Abraham as the father of faith from a spiritual perspective.

The story of Abraham helps us to interpret the meaning of faith. It is basically the response to God. Whether we talk about Abraham or any other religious person, faith is the response to God; it is this venture which provides the key to selfhood. What Abraham discovered by saying yes to God was himself, Abraham. He became aware, like the theologian Kierkegaard, that "To venture causes anxiety, but not to venture is to lose one's self . . . and to venture in the highest sense is precisely to become conscious of one's self." [1]

To respond in faith means that one becomes open to the real meaning of life. Abraham is the father of the faithful because he believed that life had worth. His response to God's call gave him meaning. Abraham's response to God involved also the risk of leaving his family and his familiar surroundings. This is a significant dimension of faith. It means stepping out—it means risking—it means trusting that the God who calls is faithful. Abraham's response is the story of one who demonstrated the sense of the possible, who opened his life to real meaning.

The picture of one who has lost this sense is seen in the play *The Iceman Cometh* by Eugene O'Neill. This drama takes place in a saloon in which the characters portray a group of alcoholics, prostitutes, and the major character, a man who goes psychotic. They can hardly recall the times in their lives when they believed in something. Abraham's response to God's call gave him something to believe in—something to do—something to be! This is the message that Israel received from Abraham—it is the message of Abraham today!

Also, the story of Abraham helps us to realize the need to affirm our lives. The author Franz Kafka tells the awesome story of a modern salesman whose life is without purpose. He has a life-style with a routine of returning from work to his comfortable home, eating the same Sunday dinner while his father goes to sleep in the midst of the dinner. This routine is so empty and meaningless that the man wakes up one morning as a cockroach. Life without purpose is just as demeaning. Abraham is the example of the man who made his life count. Thus, Abraham was called the "father of the faithful."

The story of Jacob offers us a study in the complexity of the human character. Jacob's role as one of the patriarchs corresponds to Rollo May's four stages in the consciousness of self. These are suggested for our reflection upon the life of Jacob.[2]

First, there is the stage of *innocence*. This is the stage of innocence of an infant before self-consciousness is born. Jacob, like all of us, experienced this stage. Second, there is the stage of *rebellion,* the individual's struggle to establish inner strength in his or her own right. Jacob's trickery of his brother and his father-in-law are his attempts to be free. The third stage is *ordinary consciousness of self,* the awareness by the person to see his or her errors, to be able to learn from experiences that produce guilt feelings; and to make decisions with some responsibility. Jacob experienced this in his decision to return to his home and to become reconciled with his brother. The fourth stage is *creative consciousness of self,* which May calls "ecstasy." This is what Jacob experienced at Jabbok when his name was changed from Jacob to Israel (Genesis 32: 22-28).

Joseph is included here among the patriarchs because he possessed the courage to be himself. This is the challenge that Joseph made to ancient Israel, and it is the challenge that he offers to the church which reads the book which contains the story of his life. Joseph illustrates courage in the definition of Dr. Kurt Goldstein, the neurobiologist who defines courage thusly: "Courage, in its final analysis, is nothing but an affirmative answer to the shocks of existence, which must be borne for the actualization of one's own nature."[3]

This is the message of the Joseph story: in spite of the alienation and jealousy of his brothers, the false accusation of Potiphar's wife, and the temptation to retaliate with vengeance when he had a position of power in Egypt, he had the courage to be himself. In the midst of his brothers in Egypt he could say, "I know who I am—I am Joseph, your brother."

We now turn to the biblical experience of the patriarchs.

THE EXPERIENCE

The Old Testament writers saw Abraham and the patriarchs as their common ancestors. G. W. Anderson, a British scholar, in his significant little book *The History and Religion of Israel,* points out that these stories represent the conditions of a period much earlier than that in which they were written.[4] The basic picture we get is that of a seminomadic people frequently on the move from one part of the Fertile Crescent to another. The original purpose of the texts on the patriarchs was to show that Israel comes from a common ancestor. Georg Fohrer, a contemporary German scholar, in his recent book *History of Israelite Religion,* suggests that the term "Apiru" (persons without family relations) might best describe these early Hebrews. It is connected with the Hebrew word "ibri" which means "alien" or "without legal status."[5]

Fohrer goes further to identify the patriarchs with the Semitic migrations that took place from the desert to Syria and Arabia into the Fertile Crescent. He locates the early Israelites with the fourth major wave of migration in the pre-Christian era. Thus, he sets the date for the arrival of the patriarchs around 1400–900 B.C. They were joined by other Aramaean tribes, such as the Ammonites, Moabites, and Edomites (cf. Genesis 19:30-38). Abraham and his ancestors were a part of this migration.

Theodore H. Robinson, writing in *The Interpreter's Bible,* presents a similar view of Israel's origin. Although he places the dates earlier (1800–1500 B.C.) and identifies the early Israelite migration with the third migration, he accepts the Aramaean origin of the Israelites.[6]

Also, research shows that much of the tradition of the Hebrews goes back to the Aramaean group. All of these facts substantiate the claim of the writer in Deuteronomy who affirms "my father was a homeless Aramaean" (Deuteronomy 26:5, NEB). Let us now look at the biblical texts which treat these patriarchs.

Since the purpose of our study is to treat the basic experience of the Hebrews in the pivotal periods of their history, we will focus upon the texts that relate to Abraham, Jacob, and Joseph. Even though the traditional listing of the patriarchs does not include Joseph, he is included in this chapter as an illustration of a faithful and obedient servant of God and therefore a spiritual model for his descendants. A discussion of these texts will be sufficient to help us interpret this period.

THE UNDERSTANDING
Abraham

The story of Abraham is presented in fifteen brief, distinct, yet connected narratives in the Book of Genesis. His call is pictured from the background of a divided people. Abraham is the representative of Israel. He was chosen by God to play a decisive role in the fulfillment of his purpose. He is the recipient of the promise which includes: (*a*) receiving a land, (*b*) becoming a great nation, and (*c*) mediating blessings to other people. Israel saw itself reflected in the stories of Abraham. They illustrated the essential meaning of the Yahweh-Israel relationship. All of these narratives seek to present a microcosm of Israel's faith. Israel as a community had been the recipient of the initiative, action, and purpose of God. They had responded in faith. Abraham was a model of this response. His call must be seen in this context:

Now the Lord said to Abram, "Go from your country and your kindred and your father's house to the land that I will show you. And I will make of you a great nation, and I will bless you and make your name great, so that you will be a blessing. I will bless those who bless you, and him who curses you I will curse; and by you all the families of the earth shall bless themselves." So Abram went, as the Lord had told him; and Lot went with him (Genesis 12:1-4; cf. 15:1-6, 18:9-15).

The story of Abraham was used by the Hebrew writers to illustrate God's relationship with Israel. Abraham became the model of their experience. They saw themselves as being in the same unique relationship with God as was Abraham. *The Call, The Promise,* and *The Test* were key aspects of Israel's experience.

The Call (Genesis 12:1-4)

The call of Abraham depicted Israel's call. There are several aspects of this call that need more amplification. First, note that the initiative came from God. This was unique, for the religious practices of the surrounding people emphasized the point that not only did each clan have its own god, but also that it was the responsibility of the clan *to select* its own god. The Abraham story reverses this tradition. It was God who called Abraham. Abraham responded to God's call. This point is parallel in Israel's faith. Israel saw itself as a called people, responding to divine initiative.

The Promise (Genesis 15:1-21)

Verses 1 through 6 describe a vision in which Abraham is promised great prosperity. Verses 7 through 20 emphasize the promise of the land and the covenant. The combined stories are understood to suggest that *the promise* made to Abraham was a model of God's promise to Israel. Abraham's individual experience reminded Israel that the call involved a special favor of divine prosperity. Again, this was a significant aspect of Israel's faith. This concept of God also was different from characterizations of many of the gods of the surrounding people. God takes the initiative to *bless Israel.* This is an amazing discovery. Israel is called into a unique relationship that promises blessings.

The Test (Genesis 22:1-14)

Abraham is tested to demonstrate his faithfulness. Israel is tested also. Blessings—yes! Obedience—yes! These are two sides of the same coin; Israel can expect a blessing only through obedience.

This is why this last episode is so crucial. The Israelites were not naive—neither were they irresponsible. They saw the inextricable relationship between the two—blessings are attached to obedience.

The record shows that Israel did not always act out of this understanding. Israel's life was an example of faith and unfaith—Abraham also demonstrated this tension. After having received the call and the promise, he sought to protect his life by falsifying his relationship with his wife. Abraham acts in "unfaith" (Genesis 12:10-15). Again the relationship between Abraham and Hagar in chapters 16 and 21:7-21 shows Abraham in effect denying his call, his election, and his covenant promise. Undergirding these stories is God's steadfast love, God's initiative and action for humankind in and through Abraham and Israel.

A story is told of a man who wanted a piece of ivory. When he made his desire known, he was immediately told that the only way one gets a piece of ivory is to take it from an elephant. Said the man, "It's attached to something." Thus it was with Israel's blessings. Blessings were available, but they were attached to obedience. This is the point of Abraham's test. This is why he was selected as Israel's hero. Although he struggled in the tension between faith and unfaith, he manifested obedience in his willingness to sacrifice his child, Isaac.

These experiences of call, promise, and test were a part of Israel's experience. The people of Israel *understood* Abraham as one who demonstrated in his life the kind of relationship with God that all of Israel must continue to emulate. Thus they interpreted Abraham's life as a model for the nation and thus decided to follow him as the pioneer of their faith.

Isaac

The Old Testament tradition does not give as much attention to Isaac as it does to Abraham and Jacob. Isaac is listed primarily in relation to his father Abraham and to Jacob and Esau. Isaac is the child of promise (Genesis 15:1-6; 17:15-21; 18:1-15) and is basically the connecting link between Abraham and Jacob.

Jacob

The patriarchal narratives on Jacob are treated in seventeen units. They begin with the birth of Esau and Jacob and end with

Jacob's reconciliation with his brother Esau. These stories are complex and have presented many problems for the biblical interpreter. In spite of this fact the underlying purpose is clear; just as Israel identified with Abraham in terms of the challenges of his character in the context of call, promise, and test, so they saw the ambiguity of their own lives in another historical figure. The name "Jacob" itself has some interesting interpretations. In the birth context it means "he takes by the heel as he supplants" (Genesis 25:26). However, this name sometimes appears in the form Jacob-El which could mean "Jacob is God" or "God overreaches." Whatever the true meaning of the term "Jacob-El," the story of the choice of Jacob over Esau does lend itself to the interpretation "God overreaches." At the same time this definition appeals to Israel's personification of Jacob in that in spite of its sin and unworthiness, God overreached; God selected Israel as a special people. Several of these episodes illustrate this principle.

Jacob's manipulation of persons and the consequences that followed are illustrative of his future life (cf. Genesis 25:19-34; 28:10-23).

First he tricked his brother out of his birthright by getting Esau to surrender his birthright for a cup of pottage (Genesis 25:19-34). Then he deceived his father by disguising as his brother to receive the birthright. Later he sought to exploit his father-in-law Laban by manipulating an agreement they had made to his own advantage (Genesis 30:25-43).

After this trickery he came to a point of real struggle. This prepared him for a new reality—a new name and reconciliation with his brother.

This story personifies Israel's experience. On the one hand, there is human manipulation and its consequences, and on the other hand, we have God's forbearance and forgiveness.

Jacob, the Manipulator

The two experiences in which Jacob outwitted his brother and father-in-law depict a human weakness in all of us and an attempt to use other people to achieve our own goals. This is just the opposite of what God expects. Jacob is an example of the manipulator. He used circumstances—hunger in the case of his brother and a contrived contract in the case of his father-in-law—to get his way. His philosophy seemed to be one of "I win—you lose." His goal was "to do in the other person before the other person had a chance to do him in."

The Jacob narrative goes to great length to point out the consequences of such manipulation, of attempts to play "God." Jacob was estranged from his brother, and the tension became so great that he had to leave home. Even though his blind father gave him a blessing, Jacob was so frustrated and distraught he did not fully appreciate the important blessing.

Jacob's flight from home is a classic study of alienation. He became a fugitive, and his mother sent him to her brother Laban as a way of protecting him from the wrath of his brother Esau. (Laban was both uncle and father-in-law to Jacob after Jacob married his first cousin Rachel.) However, sometimes one's behavior develops into patterns. Thus, in repeating his trick on his father-in-law Laban, by influencing the breeding habits of the cattle in order to increase his share of the flock, he eventually had to leave his father-in-law. In both cases human manipulation had dire consequences, and he had to return home.

God's Forbearance and Forgiveness

Just as the Hebrews saw blessings and obedience inextricably tied together, they also saw God's forbearance and forgiveness as the answer to human sin. Jacob knew that he had to become reconciled to his brother. However, he learned something that is the key to human experience. Human relationships are based upon divine relationship. Right relationship with God is a prerequisite for right relationship with humanity. Jacob had to "get right with God." But he learned a deeper truth—the right relationship with God requires a *new being*— a radical transformation. This is what happened to Jacob at Bethel. He realized his need of God:

> Then Jacob made a vow, saying, "If God will be with me, and will keep me in this way that I go, and will give me bread to eat and clothing to wear, so that I come again to my father's house in peace, then the Lord shall be my God, and this stone, which I have set up for a pillar, shall be God's house; and of all that thou givest me I will give the tenth to thee" (Genesis 28:20-22).

Many experiences transpired before the ultimate confrontation took place at the river Jabbok and Jacob really changed from a manipulator to an obedient child of God:

> And Jacob was left alone; and a man wrestled with him until the breaking of the day. When the man saw that he did not prevail against Jacob, he touched the hollow of his thigh; and Jacob's thigh was put out of joint as he wrestled with him. Then he said, "Let me go, for the day is breaking." But Jacob said, "I will not let you go, unless you bless me." And he said to him, "What is your name?" And he said "Jacob." Then he said, "Your name shall no more be called Jacob, but Israel, for you have striven with God and with men, and have prevailed." Then Jacob asked him, "Tell me, I pray, your name." But he said, "Why is it that you ask my name?" And there he blessed him. So Jacob called the name of the place Peniel, saying, "For I have seen God face to face, and yet my life is preserved" (Genesis 32:24-30).

Jacob's experience reflects the core of the religious experience. Jacob passed through what the theologian Alfred North Whitehead suggests are three perceptions of God. First, God is a nebulous, confusing being—a big question mark. Next, God is an enemy. Then God is seen as a friend. Jacob's experience parallels Whitehead's description. First, God was meaningless to him. His lack of any restraint demonstrated this fact. Second, the reality of his sin led to his view of God as enemy. At Jabbok he struggled with God. God was no longer enemy, but friend.

Jacob's experience is illustrative of God's forbearance and forgiveness to Israel and to us today. Although we seek to do our own thing and have our own way, when we accept God's offer of mercy and pardon, we find that God is our friend. This experience of God as forbearing and reconciling led the Hebrews to an understanding of God which undergirded their faith. God was the redeemer—the one who "buys" back, the one who forgives. "Though your sins are scarlet, they may become white as snow" (Isaiah 1:18b and c, NEB). God was faithful to his promise in spite of Israel's unfaithfulness. Abraham's seed would inherit the land; they would increase in numbers and be a blessing to the nations. Joseph, then, became a vital part of the fulfillment of God's promise to Abraham.

Joseph

The final patriarchal narrative focuses upon the story of Jacob's next to youngest son, Joseph. It begins with Joseph's alienation from his brothers and father with the result that he was sold into Egypt. The story ends with the burial of Jacob and Joseph's final acts. There are fourteen units in this story. The Joseph story is a continuation of the narrative of the patriarchs; however, in style and content it is radically different.

Some biblical scholars have suggested that the style and content of the Joseph story are likened to wisdom-type literature. In this case, Joseph is the typical wise man who manifests humility, forgiveness, and the fear of God. The story begins with an analysis of Joseph's family life. On the one hand, he has a favored status; he is the son of his father's old age by his favorite wife, Rachel. His father's gift of a splendid long-sleeved robe is a symbol of his special place. "Now Israel loved Joseph more than any other of his children, because he was the son of his old age" (Genesis 37:3). This favored status created problems for him with his brothers—"but when his brothers saw that their father loved him more than all his brothers, they hated him, and could not speak peaceably to him" (Genesis 37:4).

Two other factors influenced Joseph's family situation. One day he gave his father an unhappy report on his brothers (Genesis 37:2). This in turn intensified their feelings of hate and jealousy. Joseph's relating of his dreams was interpreted as being a bit of arrogance:

> Now Joseph had a dream, and when he told it to his brothers they only hated him the more. He said to them, "Hear this dream which I have dreamed: behold, we were binding sheaves in the field, and lo, my sheaf arose and stood upright; and behold, your sheaves gathered round it and bowed down to my sheaf." His brothers said to him, "Are you indeed to reign over us? Or are you indeed to have dominion over us?" So they hated him yet more for his dreams and for his words. Then he dreamed another dream, and told it to his brothers, and said, "Behold, I have dreamed another dream; and behold, the sun, the moon, and eleven stars were bowing down to me." But when he told it to his father and to his brothers, his father rebuked him, and said to him, "What is this dream that you have dreamed? Shall I and your mother and your brothers indeed come

to bow ourselves to the ground before you?" And his brothers were jealous of him, but his father kept the saying in mind (Genesis 37:5-11).

The next scene pictures the brothers' decision to get rid of him. Several options were suggested. First, they decided to kill him: ". . . they conspired against him to kill him. They said to one another, 'Here comes this dreamer. Come now, let us kill him and throw him into one of the pits; then we shall say that a wild beast has devoured him, and we shall see what will become of his dreams'" (Genesis 37:18b-20).

After much discussion they made the decision to sell Joseph to some of the Ishmaelite traders who were passing by, instead of killing him.

This story could be called "The Sorrows and Travails of a Young Man." Although Joseph was a slave, he was able to achieve the favor of Potiphar, an officer of Pharaoh (Genesis 39:1-6). But trouble struck again—Potiphar's wife sought to seduce Joseph. When he refused, she falsely accused him of approaching her, and he was imprisoned (Genesis 39:6-23). While in prison Joseph was able to gain the attention of the Pharaoh by his ability to interpret dreams, having successfully interpreted the dreams of the butler and baker who were in prison with him (Genesis 40:1-23). Joseph's talent in interpreting dreams enhanced his status. Later, when the Pharaoh himself needed to have his dreams interpreted, he, through the suggestion of the baker who had been released from prison, called upon Joseph. Joseph's ability to interpret the dream gave him even greater status with the Pharaoh. When he indicated to the Pharaoh that his dreams about cows and corn were warnings that there would be seven plenteous years and seven lean years, Joseph was put in charge of setting up a program to preserve the surplus from the plenteous years (Genesis 41:37-45).

Up to this point the underlying theme has been Joseph's rise to success in spite of the jealousy of his brothers, the enslavement by the Ishmaelites, and the false accusation by Potiphar's wife. There was a providential power that enabled Joseph to persevere. In spite of these obstacles Joseph achieved a position of power in Egypt.

The focus of the story shifts to Joseph's use of his power. After the dream was fulfilled, the famine hit the land. The only place where there was corn was in Egypt. Joseph was governor of the land, and his brothers came to Egypt for food.

This is where the theme of the wise man emerges. How would a person with power and influence behave? This was the test for Joseph. The other hardships were preliminary to this critical issue. This was when the questions of humility, forgiveness, and the fear of God emerged. The projection of these ideals is found in the story of Joseph.

Throughout all of this Joseph was humble. He cried when he saw his brothers: "Then Joseph could not control himself before all those who stood by him; and he cried . . ." (Genesis 45:1). He identified himself to them and said, ". . . do not be distressed or angry with yourselves, because you sold me here" (Genesis 45:5).

In one of the most moving passages of the whole episode, Joseph summarized the significance of the total situation:

". . . God sent me before you to preserve life. For the famine has been in the land these two years; and there are yet five years in which there will be neither plowing nor harvest. And God sent me before you to preserve for you a remnant on earth, and to keep alive for you many survivors. So it was not you who sent me here, but God; and he has made me a father to Pharaoh, and lord of all his house and ruler over all the land of Egypt" (Genesis 45:5-8).

This is the portrait of the wise man, the person who personifies humility, forgiveness, and the fear of God.

Obviously Israel realized that the promise to become a blessing to the nations had not been fulfilled. Nevertheless, this was a definite part of the promise. Thus, Joseph was more a projection of Israel's hopes and aspirations—a desire of what Israel might be.

THE CROSSING POINT

The patriarchs seem so far removed from our present day that we ask: How are these narratives related to our experience today?

First, the stories of the patriarchs suggest to us the basic Christian attitude toward the relationship between God and humankind. God is Creator—humankind is the creature. Humankind's response is not self-sufficiency but obedience. In the narratives found in Genesis, chapters 1 through 11, we see a general movement of humankind away from God. The climax of this is in the episode of the Tower of Babel—human self-seeking is seen at its demonic worst. The creature seeks to demonstrate self-sufficiency and independence. The story of the patriarchs began the movement of the real relationship between God and humankind. God calls—Abraham responds. God makes his promise to one who in faith responds to him. Faith is not self-sufficiency but saying "yes" to God.

Abraham's willingness to kill his son was an act of absolute faith. God's test required radical obedience, and Abraham responded in faith. Why then did Abraham do it? For God's sake and (in complete identity with this) for his own sake. He did it for God's sake because God required this proof of his faith; for his own sake he did it in order that he might furnish the proof.

This is the crossing point between Abraham and our faith today. It is the challenge to respond to God's call. It is the message that permeates the life of the patriarchs. God's call demands response. The question is whether we are ready to follow Abraham and commit ourselves to God. A modern story illustrates the kind of response Abraham made to God.

A little girl had a brother who was ill. He had a rare blood type and badly needed a blood transfusion. After a fruitless search for a donor the decision was made to ask the little girl who had the same blood type to donate blood for her critically ill brother. The little girl was shocked when first asked but finally responded favorably to the request. The doctor prepared her for the transfusion and at the appointed time withdrew the blood. After the needles had been removed from her arms, she looked up at the doctor with amazement. Bewildered, she said, "But, doctor, when am I going to die?" The little girl thought that giving blood meant she would die; yet she was willing to make the sacrifice for her brother. She was willing to demonstrate her love for her brother. Faith requires that kind of absolute surrender of the self!

QUESTIONS FOR FURTHER CONSIDERATION

• From the perspective of obedience and trust in God, how do we respond to the following problem: Scientists have developed a vaccine against diphtheria, which used to be a deadly killer of children. If we enable persons to survive instead of dying from dreadful diseases, thereby increasing population, what is the responsibility of Christians for an increased food supply for the expanded population?

• Some see Abraham as a potential murderer as he willingly offered Isaac as a living sacrifice. These persons would probably see Abraham as a mad fanatic. How does one distinguish between the person of faith and a mad fanatic?

• What is the meaning of manipulation? Is manipulation of persons ever justified? Why or why not?

The Exodus
Chapter 4

The core of the biblical faith is faithfulness to God. Many times it is not easy to see all the possibilities, but God keeps his promise. This is the basic theme in the Exodus drama. God kept his promise which he had made to Abraham. In spite of the fact that "there arose a king that did not remember Joseph's heroic service to the kings of Egypt"; although the Hebrews were made to make "brick without straw"; and even though the Hebrews were enslaved for approximately 480 years in Egypt—God kept his promise and delivered the Hebrews from bondage.

God's faithfulness is related to his covenant. The Exodus was a part of the larger understanding of Israel's relationship with God as expressed in the covenant. God took the initiative and elected Abraham and Israel to be his people. In this sense the deliverance from Egypt demonstrated God's fulfillment of his promise to Abraham and set forth the basis for the covenant relationship: "I am the Lord your God, who brought you out of the land of Egypt, out of the house of bondage" (Exodus 20:2).

Some scholars suggest at least four covenants between God and humankind in the Pentateuch: *first,* God's covenant with Adam (Genesis 1:26–2:4a); *second,* his covenant with Noah (Genesis 9:8-17); *third,* his covenant with Abraham (Genesis 17); and *fourth,* his covenant on Sinai (Exodus 19:1-6)—the climax of the Exodus event. The Exodus was the main event in the covenant relationship.

In addition to the covenant several other elements of Israel's experience speak to us with poignant relevancy. The theme "brought out of Egypt" speaks to our understanding of God as the one who delivers the oppressed. This theme was used by the early church to interpret God's deliverance of his people from the hostility of the pagan Roman emperors. The theme "the spoilation of the Egyptian" was another way of expressing this power of God over the oppressors. In the last century the black slaves in America saw in the Exodus theme a parallel to their own brutal existence in this country. The spiritual "Go Down, Moses" is illustrative of many of the spirituals which use the Exodus events as a basis for their hope of deliverance. The words of that song are vibrant with the struggle's meaning:

> Go down, Moses,
> 'Way down in Egypt's land.
> Tell old Pharaoh
> "Let my people go!"

More recently the Exodus theme has been treated in terms of liberation theology. Although the major thrust comes from the New Testament and the work of Jesus as the liberator of all of humankind, the Exodus theme serves as the background for this understanding of God as a mighty deliverer. God delivers, and he expects obedience from those he has freed. Both oppressor and oppressed are liberated to be God's people. Let us look at the Hebrew's experience and understanding of this period.

THE EXPERIENCE

A common question about the Old Testament is, "What is the starting point of Israel's history?" Did it begin with the patriarchs whom Israel saw as their common ancestors? Is the starting place the establishment of the monarchy when the tribes were welded into an organized state and the serious compilation of records began? Or is the appropriate starting place the Exodus from Egypt and the subsequent settlement of the tribes in the land of Canaan?

Strong arguments can be made for each of these starting points, and all of them represent significant "beginnings" in the life of Israel. Whichever place one begins, the story of the Exodus from Egypt and the subsequent landing in the land of Canaan is an indispensable part of Hebrew history.

When we come to the concept of God, it is clear from the biblical texts that the introduction of the name "Yahweh" by Moses marks a beginning point in Israel's history. This period of Hebrew history is complex; and many theories have been offered to locate the "Sea of

Reeds," the date when the Hebrews entered Egypt, the length of time they stayed there, the date they left Egypt, and the date they occupied the land of Canaan. However important these critical matters are, it is not within the purpose of the present author to treat these topics. Any good commentary on these books discussed will treat the passages in their context. The purpose of our discussion here is to ascertain the basic experiences of the Hebrew people during this decisive period of their history.

The main events in the Exodus are treated in seven narratives. These narratives present the basic motif in the experiences of the Hebrews—liberation from bondage. Let us look at several of them.

The Descent into Egypt

These are the names of the sons of Israel who came to Egypt with Jacob, each with his household: Reuben, Simeon, Levi, and Judah, Issachar, Zebulun, and Benjamin, Dan and Naphtali, Gad and Asher. All the offspring of Jacob were seventy persons; Joseph was already in Egypt. Then Joseph died, and all his brothers, and all that generation. But the descendants of Israel were fruitful and increased greatly; they multiplied and grew exceedingly strong; so that the land was filled with them (Exodus 1:1-7).

This narrative describes the offspring of Jacob. Three comments should be made about this text. *First,* the author is seeking to give a context for the deliverance event; thus the use of the number seventy is symbolic of the presence in Egypt of the offspring of Jacob and thus inclusive of all tribes that become Israel. *Second,* the text refers to the rapid increase of Israel. The indication here is that the promise made to Abraham is being fulfilled, even in a foreign land: "And I will make of you a great nation, and I will bless you, and make your name great, so that you will be a blessing" (Genesis 12:2). *Third,* mention of the extraordinary rapid increase of the Hebrews indicated a possible threat to the political life of Egypt. The growing number of Hebrews, "the land was filled with them," suggests the kind of potential problems this group might have posed for Egypt.

The Reversal of Egyptian Policy

Many attempts have been made to explain the phrase "new

king over Egypt" in Exodus 1:8. For the present author, the significance of this phrase is that it was the biblical writer's way of
describing a new policy toward the Hebrews:

> Now there arose a new king over Egypt, who did not know
> Joseph. And he said to his people, "Behold, the people of Israel are
> too many and too mighty for us. Come, let us deal shrewdly with
> them, lest they multiply, and, if war befall us, they join our enemies
> and fight against us and escape from the land." Therefore they set
> taskmasters over them to afflict them with heavy burdens; and they
> built for Pharaoh store-cities, Pithom and Raamses. But the more
> they were oppressed, the more they multiplied and the more they
> spread abroad. And the Egyptians were in dread of the people of
> Israel (Exodus 1:8-12).

The purpose of the enslavement was two-fold: to use this group as a
labor force and to slow down the rapid growth of the Israelites.
However, enslavement itself did not curb the fertility; so Pharaoh
tried another plan—the destruction of the sons of Israel at birth:
"Then the king of Egypt said to the Hebrew midwives, one of whom
was named Shiphrah and the other Puah, 'When you serve as midwife
to the Hebrew women, and see them upon the birthstool, if it is a son,
you shall kill him, but if it is a daughter, she shall live'" (Exodus 1:15-
16).

Moses' Call

There are two accounts of Moses' call—one is found in
Exodus 3:1–6:1; the other is found in Exodus 6:2–7:13. Most scholars
agree that the accounts are the work of two writers. The second
account supplements the first account.

The story of Moses is critical to this period; so we will look at his
life in detail. He was reared by Pharaoh's daughter, but he soon
realized that he was not Egyptian:

> One day, when Moses had grown up, he went out to his people
> and looked on their burdens; and he saw an Egyptian beating a
> Hebrew, one of his people. He looked this way and that, and seeing
> no one he killed the Egyptian and hid him in the sand (Exodus 2:11-
> 12).

His identification with the Hebrews through the violent act of murder created a crisis, and he was forced to leave Egypt. He hid for a while in the land of Midian and became a fugitive from justice (Exodus 2:16-22). He sought employment and became a shepherd with Jethro, his father-in-law, the priest of Midian.

In the first account of Moses' call (Exodus 3:1–6:1) Moses was carrying out his responsibilities as a shepherd when he was struck by the mysterious occurrence of "a bush burning but not consumed." Here God spoke to him and called his name, "Moses, Moses!" He responded, "Here am I." Then in awe he hid his face. God identified himself, "I am the God of your father, the God of Abraham, the God of Isaac, and the God of Jacob" (Exodus 3:6). Then God related to Moses his purpose:

> Then the Lord said, "I have seen the affliction of my people who are in Egypt, and have heard their cry because of their taskmasters; I know their sufferings, and I have come down to deliver them out of the hand of the Egyptians, and to bring them up out of that land to a good and broad land, a land flowing with milk and honey, to the place of the Canaanites, the Hittites, the Amorites, the Perizzites, the Hivites, and the Jebusites. And now, behold, the cry of the people of Israel has come to me, and I have seen the oppression with which the Egyptians oppress them. Come, I will send you to Pharaoh that you may bring forth my people, the sons of Israel, out of Egypt" (Exodus 3:7-10).

This vision is significant in that it emphasizes that God took the initiative. More important is the fact that this call implies that God revealed his name:

> But Moses said to God, "Who am I that I should go to Pharaoh and bring the sons of Israel out of Egypt?" He said, "But I will be with you; and this shall be the sign for you, that I have sent you: when you have brought forth the people out of Egypt, you shall serve God upon this mountain."
>
> Then Moses said to God, "If I come to the people of Israel and say to them, 'The God of your fathers has sent me to you,' and they ask me, 'What is his name?' what shall I say to them?" God said to Moses, "I AM WHO I AM." And he said, "Say this to the people of Israel, 'I AM has sent me to you.'" God also said to Moses, "Say this to the people of Israel, 'The Lord, the God of your fathers, the God

of Abraham, the God of Isaac, and the God of Jacob, has sent me to you': this is my name for ever, and thus I am to be remembered throughout all generations" (Exodus 3:11-15).

Moses here entered into a conversation with God about his plans. Moses believed that he could not lead Israel even with God's help. Who was he to assume such a responsibility? First, Moses wanted to know whose authority he had. God assured him, "I will be with you." "I AM WHO I AM" or "I will be what I will be." William Orr, Professor Emeritus of New Testament at Pittsburgh Seminary, in his commencement address at the seminary in 1973, suggested that as we tie in the name of God with the task God assigned to Moses, the text could be translated, "I will be there when you get there." Here God's name is consistent with his nature. God assured Moses that he would be with him as he fulfilled the task God gave him. God instructed Moses to go to the people and proclaim:

"The Lord, the God of your fathers, the God of Abraham, of Isaac, and of Jacob, has appeared to me, saying, 'I have observed you and what has been done to you in Egypt; and I promise that I will bring you up out of the land of the affliction of Egypt to the land of the Canaanites, the Hittites, the Amorites, the Perizzites, the Hivites, and the Jebusites, a land flowing with milk and honey'" (Exodus 3:16-17).

Then God assured Moses that the elders would receive his message. Finally, God assured Moses of the despoliation of the Egyptians:

"And I will give this people favor in the sight of the Egyptians; and when you go, you shall not go empty, but each woman shall ask of her neighbor, and of her who sojourns in her house, jewelry of silver and of gold, and clothing, and you shall put them on your sons and on your daughters; thus you shall despoil the Egyptians" (Exodus 3:21-22).

After having been given power to excel in "secret arts" then present in Egypt (Exodus 4:1-9; 17) and having been assured that Aaron could serve as his spokesman (Exodus 4:10-16), Moses returned to Egypt (Exodus 4:18-31). He was circumcised (Exodus 4:24-26), and then he began his task. He met with Aaron (Exodus 4:27-31) and shared with him his experience and God's plan. Then Moses and Aaron confronted Pharaoh: "Thus says the Lord, the God of Israel, 'Let my people go . . .'" (Exodus 5:1). Pharaoh scorned God (Exodus 5:2-5) and retaliated (Exodus 5:6-14) and even refused to listen to the pleading of a delegation of foremen to let the Israelites go (Exodus 5:15-21).

The second account of Moses' call is found in Exodus 6:2–7:13. As one compares the two accounts, there are some significant differences. In the second account there is no vision—no burning bush. Instead, there is the direct statement, "God said to Moses . . ." (Exodus 6:2-3). Another significant difference is the role of Aaron. In the first account Aaron's role is substantially less than that of Moses. In the second account a lot of care is given to the role of Aaron as a basis for the priestly tradition. However, there are no substantive differences between the two accounts with reference to the theme of deliverance. The call of Moses was a call to freedom. It was God's way of responding to the cry of an oppressed people to be freed from their bondage.

The significant point of the call of Moses is that God presents himself as deliverer. There are four words to indicate God's awareness: (a) God hears, (b) God remembers, (c) God sees, and (d) God knows. In Exodus 3:8 God shares with Moses his plan of response to the predicament of the Hebrew people. In a real way the burning bush experience can be called a confirmation of awareness. Moses knew the condition of his people as they were aware of their own circumstances. But the question was: Is God aware, or is he secluded in the confines of his own sanctuary? If he is aware, what is he going to do about our oppression? God's call to Moses through the burning bush answers these questions. God identified himself as a liberator. He said, "I have come down to deliver them" (v. 8). Thus, God through Moses was saying that he was already engaged in the process of deliverance.

It is significant that the root of the word "deliver" means to snatch away. God was saying to Moses, "I have come down to snatch you away from Egypt and to deliver you to the Promised Land." *God took the initiative.* His call to Moses was a part of God's role as Redeemer. This concept of God was also expressed in the words of the psalmist: "The Lord executeth righteousness and judgment for all that are oppressed" (Psalm 103:6,KJV). The God of Moses was a God of action, on behalf of the oppressed.

The Plagues

God's activity was seen in the plagues—instruments to convince Pharaoh to allow the children of Israel to leave Egypt. There were two ways of viewing the plagues. One is the traditional way of seeing them as only supernatural events, direct intervention by God to effect deliverance from Egypt and bondage. The second view, which is held by some modern biblical scholars, is that the plagues were natural events which occurred frequently in Egypt between July (when the Nile began to overflow its banks) and the following April. The latter view does not deny the providential character of these natural events as they relate to the deliverance of the Israelites from bondage, but it does reflect the growing knowledge of natural science. The neighbors of the Hebrews saw elements of nature as either friendly or hostile insofar as they directly benefited or suffered from their effects. But the Hebrews, through divine revelation, understood that God controlled all natural forces and used them for his own design. All nature was under God's control and subject to divine plans. Thus the viewing of the plagues as natural events in no way minimizes God's omnipotence. The plagues were a part of an infinite design. The record, as we have it, is the work of an editor who has woven them together in a dramatic way. The final list, as we have it, gives them as follows:

1. The Water Turned to Blood (7:14-24)
2. Frogs (7:25-8:14)
3. Gnats (8:16-18)
4. Flies (8:20-31)
5. Pestilence (9:1-7)
6. Boils (9:8-12)
7. Hail (9:13-35)
8. Locusts (10:1-20)
9. Darkness (10:21-29)
10. Death of the Firstborn (11:1-10)

The first four are traceable to the inundation of the Nile. Basically they were annoyances. The next four caused damage to persons and property. The ninth caused terror, and the tenth brought consternation. The writer of the narrative saw these plagues as evidence of God's omnipotence (Exodus 7:14-19). The most serious plague was the death of the firstborn. It was the final catastrophe (Exodus 12:1–13:16). Although Pharaoh seemed set in his decision to keep them in bondage, God prepared them to leave (Exodus 12:1–13:16).

The announcement of the catastrophic decree of death of the firstborn (Exodus 11:1-10) was followed by the actual event, described in 12:29-32:

> At midnight the Lord smote all the first-born in the land of Egypt, from the first-born of Pharaoh who sat on his throne to the first-born of the captive who was in the dungeon, and all the first-born of the cattle. And Pharaoh rose up in the night, he, and all his servants, and all the Egyptians; and there was a great cry in Egypt, for there was not a house where one was not dead. And he summoned Moses and Aaron by night, and said, "Rise up, go forth from among my people, both you and the people of Israel; and go, serve the Lord, as you have said. Take your flocks and your herds, as you have said, and be gone; and bless me also!"

Journey to the Mount of God

Following the dedication of the firstborn, an act of commitment and thanksgiving (Exodus 13:1-2, 11-16), the Israelites departed from Egypt. This was not an easy way, "but God led the people round by the way of the wilderness toward the Red Sea" (Exodus 13:18). They went from Succoth to Etham (Exodus 13:20-22). The author describes their journey aptly:

> And they moved on from Succoth, and encamped at Etham, on the edge of the wilderness. And the Lord went before them by day in a pillar of cloud to lead them along the way, and by night in a pillar of fire to give them light, that they might travel by day and by night; the pillar of cloud by day and the pillar of fire by night did not depart from before the people (Exodus 13:20-22).

Their trip was not without difficulties. God presented Moses with strange orders (Exodus 14:1-4). Their precarious position frightened the Israelites and they cried out, "Is it because there are no graves in Egypt that you have taken us away to die in the wilderness?" (Exodus 14:11). Moses challenged them with the words, "Fear not, stand firm,

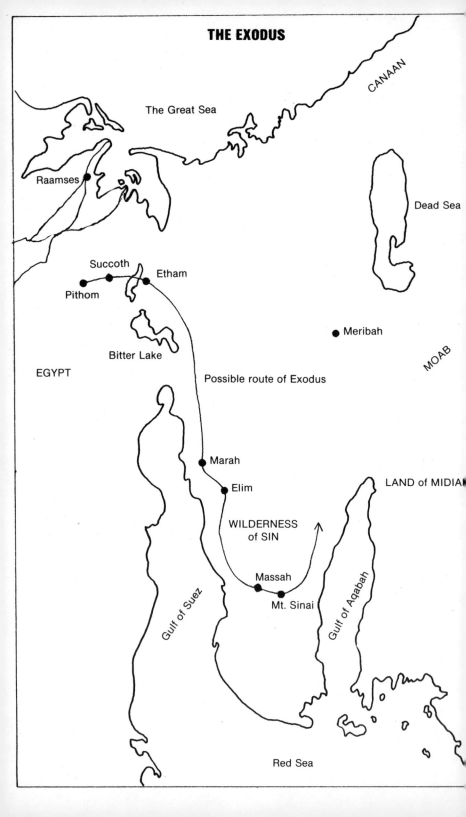

and see the salvation of the Lord, which he will work for you today; for the Egyptians whom you see today, you shall never see again" (Exodus 14:13).

In obedience to God they marched forward and crossed the Red Sea:

> The Lord said to Moses, "Why do you cry to me? Tell the people of Israel to go forward. Lift up your rod, and stretch out your hand over the sea and divide it, that the people of Israel may go on dry ground through the sea. And I will harden the hearts of the Egyptians so that they shall go in after them, and I will get glory over Pharaoh and all his host, his chariots, and his horsemen. And the Egyptians shall know that I am the Lord, when I have gotten glory over Pharaoh, his chariots, and his horsemen."
>
> Then the angel of God who went before the host of Israel moved and went behind them; and the pillar of cloud moved from before them and stood behind them, coming between the host of Egypt and the host of Israel. And there was the cloud and the darkness; and the night passed without one coming near the other all night.
>
> Then Moses stretched out his hand over the sea; and the Lord drove the sea back by a strong east wind all night, and made the sea dry land, and the waters were divided. And the people of Israel went into the midst of the sea on dry ground, the waters being a wall to them on their right hand and on their left (Exodus 14:15-22).

The Egyptian soldiers were drowned as they sought to pursue the Israelites. As an act of praise and honor of God the Israelites sang two victory hymns, the Song of Moses (Exodus 15:1-18) and the Song of Miriam (Exodus 15:21). The Song of Miriam celebrated the escape and was probably written much earlier. The Song of Moses celebrated the protection of God for the Israelites during the pilgrimage in the wilderness and presupposes the establishment of the temple in Israel.

The last set of experiences was encountered during the journey to Sinai (Exodus 15:22-18:27). Although the Israelites had been delivered from Egypt, they still had to face crises which grew out of thirst, hunger, and lack of security. In every case God supported Moses' leadership. At Marah the bitter water was made sweet (Exodus 15:23-25); at Elim they found water and palm trees (Exodus 15:27); in the wilderness of Sin they found manna (Exodus 16:1-36); and at Massah and Meribah, Moses in anger struck a rock to give them water when they murmured a third time about their thirst (Exodus 17:1-7).

THE UNDERSTANDING

The question now arises as to the Israelites' understanding of the Exodus. One of the earliest interpretations is the Song of Miriam:

> For when the horses of Pharaoh with his chariots and his horsemen went into the sea, the Lord brought back the waters of the sea upon them; but the people of Israel walked on dry ground in the midst of the sea. Then Miriam, the prophetess, the sister of Aaron, took a timbrel in her hand; and all the women went out after her with timbrels and dancing. And Miriam sang to them:
>
> > "Sing to the Lord, for he has triumphed gloriously;
> > the horse and his rider he has thrown into the sea."
> > (Exodus 15:19-21)

This song celebrates the victory of God in delivering the Hebrews from bondage. This song was echoed years later in the Negro spiritual: "Oh, Mary, don't you weep, don't you mourn, Pharaoh's army got drowned. Oh, Mary, don't you weep."

The destruction of the Egyptian army was a graphic image in the Hebrew understandings of the Exodus. Martin Noth has indicated at least three themes that were emphasized very early in the Israelite understanding of Exodus.[1] First, they understood that Israel was brought out of Egypt. Several passages express this view (cf. Numbers 23:22-24; 24:8; 1 Samuel 4:8; 2 Samuel 7:23). These passages emphasize that the heart of Israel's faith began with an awareness that she was a captive, oppressed people in a foreign land. In all these texts the emphasis was about Israel as the recipient of God's favor. The philosopher Martin Buber expressed this same belief when he wrote concerning the Exodus: "What is decisive with respect to the inner history of Mankind, however, is that the children of Israel understood this as an act of their God, as a 'miracle'; which does not mean that they interpreted it as a miracle, but that they experienced it as such, that as such they perceived it."[2]

Another tradition which was a part of Israel's understanding of this period was the relationship between the patriarchs and the Exodus. For the Israelites the deliverance was God's fulfillment of his promise to Abraham, Isaac, and Jacob (cf. Genesis 12:7). This relationship between the patriarchs and the Exodus gave a theological explanation for Israel as a people of God in the land which its God had given to it. This understanding was critical, not only for ancient Israel but it also is for Israel today. Undergirding this understanding is the belief that the land of Palestine was God's gift to Israel in fulfillment of the promise to Abraham.

Still another understanding which the Israelites developed from their experience in this period was the inextricable relationship between freedom and responsibility. This was expressed concretely in the covenant at Sinai. This covenant had the effect of binding Israel to the God who had delivered them out of Egypt. It is clear that through this experience the "God of the fathers" became the God of Israel. Whatever the historical details might have been, Noth contends, ". . . the God who appeared in Sinai is, needless to say, the same as the God who showed his power in the deliverance 'by the sea.'"[3] Yahweh is the God who called Moses (cf. Exodus 3:1-6).

The Israelites understood that Yahweh was the same God who now invited them into a covenant relationship with him. The acceptance of the covenant relationship demanded wholehearted loyalty to God. J. Coert Rylaarsdam has described the significance of the covenant in Israel: "The covenant is the central implementation of the faith which constituted Israel's response to the Exodus. It is the symbol that describes the relationship in which Yahweh and his people stand to one another."[4]

The enactment of the covenant was a significant part of the Exodus experience. The fact that the writers devoted five chapters to the giving of the covenant indicates the importance of this event in Israel's life. First there was the invitation (Exodus 19:1-8). These verses are a part of the theophany in which God appeared to Moses and Moses served as the mediator between Israel and God. God identified himself by his acts and invited Israel to obey him and be his people. They replied affirmatively. Following their response, God prepared the people for the enactment of the covenant.

God appeared on the third day, enveloped in fire (Exodus 19:16-

25). They were awed as they prepared to receive the covenant. The covenant was God's willingness to enter into a relationship with a special historical people who would obey his voice and do his will. In such a context God spoke. One hears the echo of Habakkuk: "The Lord is in his holy temple, let all the earth keep silence before him" (Habakkuk 2:20).

This brings us to the Decalogue (Exodus 20:1-17) and the Covenant Code (Exodus 20:22–23:23). These two pieces of legislation are interspersed between acceptance of the covenant and the ceremonial meal which was to seal the covenant. Let us look at these laws briefly.

In the Decalogue we have ten general statements—ten words in which the general prerogatives of God, parents, and fellow Israelites are affirmed (Exodus 20:1-17; cf. Deuteronomy 5:6-24; Exodus 34:10-26).

The Covenant Code is different in style and form. Its focus is upon the specific application of the general statements in the Decalogue. The major discussion is devoted to the social code which treats the following: (a) the Israelite slave (Exodus 21:2-11); (b) capital offenses (Exodus 21:12-17); (c) non-capital offenses/crimes (Exodus 21:18-22); (d) law securing property rights (Exodus 21:33-22:17); (e) capital offenses (Exodus 22:18-20); (f) human and (g) pious duties (Exodus 22:21-31). Undergirding all of these laws is the spirit of justice (Exodus 23:1-9).

These ideas mentioned here are more fully developed in the classical prophets: Amos, Hosea, Micah, and Isaiah (chapter 8). The code also presents the liturgical calendar including the sabbaths (Exodus 23:10-13) and the great festivals. The giving of the Decalogue and the Covenant Code is evidence of Israel's understanding that the covenant relationship had two focal points: God's care and concern, and Israel's faithfulness to him as expressed in the law. These laws were instructions or teachings for the liberated. Another way of viewing this covenant relationship is to see that God is king and Israel his subjects. Thus Israel is made a holy people—a liberated people.

THE CROSSING POINT

The Exodus is to the Hebrew faith what the incarnation is to the Christian faith. The crossing point is that both events are interpretations of historical facts as well as biblical themes. Both events affirm the belief that God who is Creator is also active in history. God acted mightily in delivering the Hebrews out of Egyptian bondage. He acted decisively (once and for all) in the sending of his Son, Jesus Christ! A cardinal affirmation of the Christian faith is that God acted in history.

This affirmation leads to the awareness that God acts in our history. History is the arena of divine action. This is what we as Christians believe about God. He acted himself in Hebrew history and in Jesus Christ. Also, we believe that God acts today in our lives. The Holy Spirit enables us to see God's manifestation of himself.

The belief that God acts in history is related to the Exodus theme that the nature of this action is liberation. The fact of the Exodus was interpreted by the Hebrews in terms of liberation. God delivered the Hebrews out of Egyptian bondage. The Christian faith interprets the coming of Christ in terms of liberation. Christ is the Liberator, the Redeemer of humankind. He liberates persons from the bondage that reduces them from the status of the image of God in which they were created. God's action in Christ is the fulfillment of the Exodus theme.

The theme of liberation is a topic of current debate in theological circles today. One of its chief exponents is Gustavo Gutiérrez, who sees the roots of liberation theology in the Exodus. He argues that creation in the Christian understanding demands liberation. He states: "The liberation from Egypt—both a historical fact and at the same time a fertile Biblical theme—enriches this vision and is moreover its true source. The creative act is linked, almost identified with, the act which freed Israel from slavery in Egypt."[5] This is a crossing point between the theme of liberation and the Old Testament Exodus. The focus is upon human liberation, the freeing of all persons to be human. The Hebrews celebrated liberation; the early Christians' proclamation of liberation in Christ and our struggle for liberation today are one basic theme. God is the source of liberation. He makes all persons free!

Another crossing point is the meaning of covenant in Israel and in the Christian faith. Deliverance and covenant were inextricably related in Israel's understanding of the Exodus. God brought them out in order that he might bring them into a land in which the covenant relationship would be realized. They were called to respond in faithfulness and trust.

The church sees itself as the new Israel; the incarnation is God's enactment of a new covenant, the calling of a people to accept his love through his Son, Jesus Christ. Covenant for the Christian involves God's initiative and challenges us to respond. This is the significant point of the covenant—it demands responsible action. To accept Christ as Lord is to follow him.

Beyond this sense of covenant as responsible action is the church's insistence that Jesus is the mediator of a new covenant. We are the new Israel because we have a new Moses. The terms of this covenant are radically different. It is not based upon law, but acceptance of God's acceptance of us, or as Tillich puts it, "to accept acceptance." This is the new covenant—God says to us in Christ, "You are accepted. You are my son—my daughter—my child!" Christ who frees us from bondages calls us into covenant with God!

QUESTIONS FOR FURTHER CONSIDERATION

• Is liberation a theme related to a particular segment of today's society, or is liberation a concern of every Christian?

• Is what way is one's existence in modern American society an evidence of bondage? From what are we to be liberated? For what are we to be liberated?

• How does the message of Christ speak to the specific kinds of bondage felt by different sections of our nation, such as high taxes, sexism, racism, crime, societal norms, and the like?

• How can the phrase "people of God" be meaningful in a pluralistic society such as the one in which we live today?

The Conquest
and Settlement
Chapter 5

When I was a little boy, the circus was a big event and was preceded by a parade with bands, elephants, and clowns. The parade engendered our excitement and enthusiasm; yet we knew that the real event—the circus—was coming. The parade announced the circus! This is the feeling that we get as we study the period of the conquest and settlement. It was a time of excitement—Jericho, Joshua, the Judges, Gideon, Jephthah—but really it was a prelude, an anticipation, a great expectation. The curtains are drawn, the audience is hushed, and the performance is ready to begin. The main events of this period demand careful scrutiny.

The conquest and settlement are part of the formative period of Israel's history. In this chapter the discussion of these two events has been separated for purposes of clarity and focus since the process of experience and understanding took on a somewhat different focus for each.

THE CONQUEST

We have already seen that the documents from this early period in Israelite history are complex and are the result of diverse sources. The Bible does give us some evidence by which an historical base for understanding the principal developments can be developed. John Bright, in his book *A History of Israel,* has suggested a possible reconstruction of these events which may be helpful here. His outline reads:

    a) Preconquest Occupation—semi-nomadic migrations to Palestine early in the second millennium.
    b) Egyptian Bondage and Exodus—subsequent bondage of the Israelites and their liberation from Egypt.

c) The Conquest and Absorption—the Israelites' movement from Sinai to Kadesh and after a period of wandering, final settlement in Palestine.[1]

This chapter's focus is the experience of the Israelites during the conquest and absorption. These questions emerge as we investigate the conquest: What are the main events? Who were the major leaders? What methods or plans did they follow? What difficulties did they encounter, both externally and internally? What were the results?

The Experience

There are several options about Israel's conquest of the land. Some suggest that it was a unified attack which took place at one particular time—the kind of invasion that took place when the Allied forces invaded Normandy in World War II. Others suggest that it took place gradually; that is, one by one, sections of Palestine fell under the domination of Israel. Still others question the biblical narrative by asking whether the stories are based on actual history or legends which explain the origins of worship sites.

The evidence in the Scriptures suggests that at least two invasions took place. First, the Israelites moved to the highlands east of the Jordan occupied by the kingdom of the Heshbon and destroyed it (Numbers 21:21-32). This secured for them the territory between the Arnon and the Jabbok (v. 24). Later they conquered most of the Transjordanian uplands. Another set of invasions which focused upon western Palestine took place later. These are the traditional stories of the conquest which one finds in the book of Joshua. In these battles, God is pictured as the one who fulfills his promise by giving them a homeland.

The Events

The key events described in the Book of Joshua suggest that Israel prepared for the conquest through the sending of spies (2:1-24). Following the crossing of the Jordan (3:1-5:1), they performed rites of circumcision and the Passover at Gilgal prior to the fall of Jericho. The battle presented in classic detail merits special attention because it gives us insight into how this experience was seen as evidence of God's presence and power. First, there was the voice of God addressing Joshua and the people (5:13-15). The commander of the Lord's army appeared as a prelude to the event:

When Joshua was by Jericho, he lifted up his eyes and looked, and behold, a man stood before him with his drawn sword in his hand; and Joshua went to him and said to him, "Are you for us, or for our adversaries?" And he said, "No; but as commander of the army of the Lord I have now come." And Joshua fell on his face to the earth, and worshiped, and said to him, "What does my Lord bid his servant?" And the commander of the Lord's army said to Joshua, "Put off your shoes from your feet; for the place where you stand is holy." And Joshua did so (Joshua 5:13-15).

This is similar to Moses' assurance that God would lead Israel out of Egypt. Joshua, like Moses, removed his sandals in recognition of divine presence. Then he received instructions:

Now Jericho was shut up from within and from without because of the people of Israel; none went out, and none came in. And the Lord said to Joshua, "See, I have given into your hand Jericho, with its king and mighty men of valor. You shall march around the city, all the men of war going around the city once. Thus shall you do for six days. And seven priests shall bear seven trumpets of rams' horns before the ark; and on the seventh day you shall march around the city seven times, the priests blowing the trumpets. And when they make a long blast with the ram's horn, as soon as you hear the sound of the trumpet, then all the people shall shout with a great shout; and the wall of the city will fall down flat, and the people shall go up every man straight before him" (Joshua 6:1-5).

These instructions included both religious (ritualistic) and military instructions. "Seven priests shall bear seven trumpets of rams' horns" suggests the character of this experience. The conquest of Jericho was interpreted as a demonstration of their obedience to God rather than an armed struggle. They believed God had already assured them: "I have delivered Jericho and her king into your hands" (Joshua 6:2, NEB). The execution of the divine order was carried out in the battle (Joshua 6:6-27). The final narrative (Joshua 6:14-25) treats the destruction of the city and Joshua's order to save Rahab's house because of her assistance to the spies who preceded Joshua.

The next event is presented in sharp contrast to the victory at Jericho. At first, Israel was defeated at Ai because Achan violated the ban to destroy all spoils of war. He was punished along with his family in the Valley of Achor (Joshua 7:1-26). This was followed then by a victory (Joshua 8:1-29).

The final section of the conquest narrative describes its completion (Joshua 9:1-11:23). The main purpose of these chapters is to show how the conquest, having begun with Jericho and Ai, spread from the hill country (chapter 9) through Canaan (chapter 10) to the north (chapter 11). The final summary of the conquest provides an overall view of these experiences:

So Joshua took all that land, the hill country and all the Negeb and all the land of Goshen and the lowland and the Arabah and the hill country of Israel and its lowland from Mount Halak, that rises toward Seir, as far as Baalgad in the valley of Lebanon below Mount Hermon. And he took all their kings, and smote them, and put them to death (Joshua 11:16-17).

The Leaders

So far we have presented the main events in the conquest. Let us now look at the major leaders. The tradition of the Israelites placed the primary leadership role upon Joshua. This tradition assumes that there was a major invasion and that Joshua was the leader. This approach has been seriously questioned by recent scholars who have studied the early Israelite history. Among these is John Bright (who follows Martin Noth, the German Old Testament scholar), suggesting that the political structure of early Israel was not a racial or national unit, as has been generally assumed, but a loose confederation of clans, which were united under a covenant with God. He further argues that the scheme for this affiliation came from the stories of the twelve sons of Jacob: Reuben, Simeon, Levi, Judah, Issachar, and Zebulun by Leah, Gad and Asher by Leah's slave Zilpah, Joseph and Benjamin by Rachel, and Dan and Naphtali by Bilhah, Rachel's slave.

Bright feels that this confederation was organized during the time of the wilderness journey, at least by the time of the covenant at Sinai. Thus during the time of conquest these tribes were organized in this sacred league. Following the lead of Bright, it seems plausible to assume that the conquest was gradual although part of an overall strategy. In this sense the version in Judges seems more reasonable. There the heroic leaders included the leader of the tribes of Judah and Simeon as well as Joshua.

There were several strategies that the Israelites employed in conquest. After having secured the highland east of the Jordan, they proceeded to Jericho and Ai which were centrally located. According to the stories in Joshua they conquered the central highland, destroying or expelling the population in the process, and gave this area to the clans of Ephraim and Manasseh (named after Joseph's two sons) and Judah. After overcoming Canaanite resistance, each tribe sought to occupy its portion and engaged in a separate war of ousting the remaining Canaanites on its own.

Although Joshua had hoped to conquer the land to the Mediterranean Sea and the Euphrates River (Joshua 1:2-6), this goal was not reached. Many barriers stood in the way. One was the resistance by the Canaanites. At first this was minimal, but later the Canaanites fought tenaciously to hold their land. As resistance continued, the Israelites invoked *herem,* a practice that seems morally questionable. This practice was one of destroying in the name of God all that was a potential threat to the purity of the religious life of the Israelites. Once a city-state had been conquered, they proceeded to destroy the population as well. Both Jericho and Ai are examples of this practice. Even so there is a question as to whether the Canaanites were destroyed and expelled, or whether the Hebrews became assimilated with them. In light of the fact that total conquest was not complete (Joshua 13:1-7) and that a later interpretation by a writer indicated that Israel did not complete the conquest due to her sin, it is clear that some destruction took place, but also it seems likely that some amalgamation took place.

This brings us to the final question—what were the results? It seems that the following summary can be made of the experience of the attempt by Israel to possess the land. According to Joshua, chapters 1 through 12, it was a unified effort which involved lightning-like action that was violently brutal. The Israelites crossed the Jordan, tumbled the walls of Jericho, marched through the center of the land and then through the south and to the north. Nevertheless, all of Palestine was not conquered.

The Understanding

Israel's understanding of this period of her history is found primarily in the Book of Joshua. We have already mentioned that they saw Joshua's succession to Moses as a continuation of God's promise to bring them to the Promised Land. Therefore, the events of the conquests were interpreted in the same way. First, God chose Moses and then God chose Joshua. The details depicted in the two stories of the fall of Jericho and Achan's sin illustrate the fact that Israel saw her conquest of Canaan as a part of God's plan. The emphasis in these stories is upon God's power and might. It is also clear that the Israelites believed that the key to victory was their faithful adherence to God's plans.

The first part of chapter 24 gives Joshua's review of the mighty acts of God which had already been demonstrated (Joshua 24:1-13). Then Joshua challenged the people to choose their God. He called upon them to use the historical experiences of the Hebrew people to make their decisions:

"Now therefore fear the Lord, and serve him in sincerity and in faithfulness; put away the gods which your fathers served beyond the River, and in Egypt, and serve the Lord. And if you be unwilling to serve the Lord, choose this day whom you will serve, whether the gods your fathers served in the region beyond the River, or the gods of the Amorites in whose land you dwell; but as for me and my house, we will serve the Lord" (Joshua 24:14-15).

Finally, we have the climactic moment in which the people responded: "And the people said to Joshua, 'Nay; but we will serve the Lord'" (Joshua 24:21). The people responded at Shechem saying as they did at Mount Sinai: "Yahweh is our God—we are God's people."

John Bright has pointed out that the Book of Joshua is important not only as a record of historical events, but also as a statement of the way in which the people of the Old Testament responded to the questions: "Does God reveal himself in history? Is history the story of God's dealing with us?"[2] To these questions the Old Testament gives an affirmative answer. The dramatic acts of God were manifested through the human instrumentality, for example, of Rahab's protection of the informer, Achan's disobedience to wartime ethics, and Joshua's leadership at Jericho. God also worked through nature by drying up the waters of the Jordan, the destruction of the walls of Jericho, and the hailstones which fell upon the five Amorite kings who sought to punish Gibea. Divine Providence is seen in the whole story of the conquest and the assignment of the land to Israel.

Israel's understanding is also seen in the covenant at Shechem (Joshua 24:1-25). This covenant reflects another view of the Israelites' understanding that they were God's people and he was their God.

THE SETTLEMENT
The Experience

The writer of Judges recounts for us the experiences of this period in Israel's history. They involved the time of adjustment to their new environment in the occupied territories and the ventures and conquest of the unconquered land. At this time in their history they were basically seminomadic, and the settlement provided the transition to an agrarian way of life.

This period was characterized by charismatic leaders who, when confronted by crisis, led the people out of difficulty and then returned to obscurity. These leaders were called the "judges." They were Othniel (Judges 3:7-11), Ehud (Judges 3:12-30), Shamgar (Judges 3:31), Deborah and Barak (Judges 4:1-5:31), Gideon (Judges 6:1-8:35), Tola (Judges 10:1-2), Jair (Judges 10:3-16), Jephthah (Judges 11:11-12:7), Ibzan (Judges 12:8-10), Elon (Judges 12:11-12), and Abdon (Judges 12:13-15). The perspective for all of these judges is found in the biblical sequence: Israel was threatened. Israel cried to God and he raised up a deliverer. There was no consistent pattern of leadership—rather, different styles of leadership emerged. Othniel was the first judge. He rose to leadership during the invasion of Cushan-rishathaim of Aram-Maharaim. We are not given a lot of details about this encounter. A little more information is given about Ehud who fought the Moabites. Shamgar is listed as the third judge who was not an Israelite but probably a city king of Beth-anath in Gilead, who led an invasion against the Philistines.

We are given more detail about Deborah and Barak. Two chapters are devoted to their leadership. Three points of significance are related in these stories. First, we have the mention of a significant role by a woman who took the initiative in challenging her own nation to defend itself against the Canaanites:

Now Deborah, a prophetess, the wife of Lappidoth, was judging Israel at that time. She used to sit under the palm of Deborah between Ramah and Bethel in the hill country of Ephraim; and the people of Israel came up to her for judgment (Judges 4:4-5).

Then she forced Barak to join her in this defense:

> She sent and summoned Barak the son of Abinoam from Kedesh in Naphtali, and said to him, "The Lord, the God of Israel, commands you, 'Go, gather your men at Mount Tabor, taking ten thousand from the tribe of Naphtali and the tribe of Zebulun. And I will draw out Sisera, the general of Jabin's army, to meet you by the river Kishon with his chariots and his troops; and I will give him into your hand.'" Barak said to her, "If you will go with me, I will go; but if you will not go with me, I will not go." And she said, "I will surely go with you; nevertheless, the road on which you are going will not lead to your glory, for the Lord will sell Sisera into the hand of a woman." Then Deborah arose, and went with Barak to Kedesh (Judges 4:6-9).

The result was the defeat of the Canaanites (Judges 4:10-16). The second significant point is that a natural event provided the instrument of defeat. An unexpected rainstorm stalled the chariots of the Canaanites and thereby permitted Israel to kill the chariot riders and obtain victory. A third factor was the victory song which Deborah sang in celebration of the triumph. This song, one of the oldest pieces of poetry in the Old Testament, reveals how the people interpreted the victory.

One of the best-known judges is Gideon (Judges 6:1–8:35). His story joins with Samson as the longest stories of the Judges. Gideon's leadership emerged during the crisis of the Midianites (Judges 6:1-6). Gideon responded to a call that is described in two phases. In one call he was visited by a divine messenger (Judges 6:11-24) while he was threshing grain in a wine press.

The second phase of his call recounts the direct word from God to Gideon with instructions to break down the altar of Baal (Judges 6:25-32). Gideon, like Moses, was hesitant to assume such an awesome responsibility and demanded a test. He needed assurance that God wanted him to lead his people (Judges 6:36-40).

The narrative continued with the preparation for the battle (Judges 7:1-8) and included a strange command for testing out the soldiers who were ready for battle:

And the Lord said to Gideon, "The people are still too many; take them down to the water and I will test them for you there; and he of whom I say to you, 'This man shall go with you,' shall go with you; and any of whom I say to you, 'This man shall not go with you,' shall not go." So he brought the people down to the water; and the Lord said to Gideon, "Every one that laps the water with his tongue, as a dog laps, you shall set by himself; likewise every one that kneels down to drink." And the number of those that lapped, putting their hands to their mouths, was three hundred men; but all the rest of the people knelt down to drink water (Judges 7:4-6).

The explicitness of the instructions was similar to the instructions to Joshua on the eve of the battle of Jericho. The point was to make sure that Israel realized that "the deliverance is an act of God." "With the three hundred men that lapped I will deliver you and give the Midianites into your hands . . ." (Judges 7:7). Under God's leadership Gideon was successful and the Midianites were routed. As in the other stories of Judges, victory came through obedience to God.

Two other persons deserve special attention as we seek to present the experience of Israel in this period. One is the story of Jephthah (Judges 11:5-12:7), and the other is found in the tales related to Samson (Judges 13:1-16:31). In each of these stories the focus is different. Although the circumstance of threat from surrounding city-states is continued, other aspects of the judges' experience are emphasized. Jephthah is presented as a mighty warrior (Judges 11:1-3). He led Israel into war against the Ammonites. On the brink of the battle he made an oath of sacrifice as a sign of his appreciation for God's mighty deliverance:

Then the Spirit of the Lord came upon Jephthah, and he passed through Gilead and Manasseh, and passed on to Mizpah of Gilead, and from Mizpah of Gilead he passed on to the Ammonites. And Jephthah made a vow to the Lord, and said, "If thou wilt give the Ammonites into my hand, then whoever comes forth from the doors of my house to meet me, when I return victorious from the Ammonites, shall be the Lord's, and I will offer him up for a burnt offering." So Jephthah crossed over to the Ammonites to fight against them; and the Lord gave them into his hand. And he smote them from Aroer to the neighborhood of Minnith, twenty cities, and as far as Abelkeramim, with a very great slaughter. So the Ammonites were subdued before the people of Israel (Judges 11:29-33).

As it developed, the first person who greeted Jephthah upon his return from battle was his daughter.

> Then Jephthah came to his home at Mizpah; and behold his daughter came out to meet him with timbrels and with dances; she was his only child; beside her he had neither son nor daughter. And when he saw her, he rent his clothes, and said, "Alas, my daughter! you have brought me very low, and you have become the cause of great trouble to me; for I have opened my mouth to the Lord, and I cannot take back my vow" (Judges 11:34-35).

Samson's role in this period of Israel's history is also found in the Book of Judges. The stories about Samson illustrate Hebrew storytelling at its best. This time the enemies were the Philistines. These stories are introduced with the implication that Israel's troubles were caused by their sin: "And the people of Israel again did what was evil in the sight of the Lord" (Judges 13:1). Israel again had been unfaithful to the Lord (see Judges 2:1-5).

The story of Samson begins with the extraordinary circumstances surrounding his birth. It was foretold by an angelic visitor who told his mother (the wife of Manoah) that she would conceive and bear a son who would be a Nazarite and who would not cut his hair. His parents prayed for guidance (Judges 13:8), and their request was granted (Judges 13:15-23).

After a report of his actual birth, the author recounted that "the Spirit of the Lord began to stir him in Mahanehdan . . ." (Judges 13:25). Next, the author presented several episodes in Samson's life: (a) his first love (Judges 14:1-4); (b) the slaying of the lion (Judges 14:5-9); (c) his marriage (Judges 14:10-20); (d) his return home (Judges 15:1-8); (e) his arrest and retaliation (Judges 15:9-20); (f) his experience with the harlot of Gaza (Judges 16:1-3); and (g) his relationship with Delilah (Judges 16:4-22). These episodes present Samson as a person of superhuman strength.

The significance of the story of Samson and Delilah is its focus upon Delilah's constant attempt to learn the secret of his strength, Samson's final submission to Delilah, and its consequences. It was through her persistence that the Philistines were able to curb Samson's activity. At Timnah, his first wife had learned the secret of his riddle (Judges 14:10-18), but Delilah learned the secret of his strength (Judges 16:16-17). This revelation was the beginning of Samson's downfall. The Philistines, knowing his weakness, began to celebrate to Dagon for their victory. However, Samson's hair grew back and with it his strength. In an act of desperation he destroyed the house where the Philistines were and in the process killed himself (Judges 16:23-31). Thus the tragic story of Samson illustrates the experience of Israel when she disobeyed God. At least this was Israel's understanding of it.

There were at least two discernible trends which the Israelites developed during this period; both of them related to adaptations with the Canaanite environment. One was the emphasis upon cultic observance and the other was the adaptation of Canaanite law. The adoption of cultic practices is seen in the expansion of the number of sanctuaries or high places. Many of these were originally associated with Canaanite sanctuaries, but later they were used by Israelites to honor God. The best-known shrine is in Shiloh. During this period the Ark (a box or chest with unknown content which was brought by the Israelites across the Jordan) was placed at the shrine at Shiloh. The decision to place the Ark there was apparently to reduce defections from the worship of the God of Israel. Cultic sacrifices were offered by priests associated with the shrines (Gideon—Judges 6; Manoah—Judges 13). They also celebrated the three feasts: the Feast of Unleavened Bread, the Feast of Harvest (Feast of Weeks), and the Feast of Booths.

The second trend of the Israelites in this period was the adaptation of Canaanite law. Although one cannot easily separate the periods when different laws were adopted (especially since they were transmitted orally), it is reasonable to assume that laws developed in a seminomadic state would not suffice for a settled agrarian community. Therefore, it seems highly probable that sections of the covenant code came from Canaanite law. Israel's decision was to codify its laws and cultic practices under the influence of Canaanite environment. This decision was to cause dire consequences.

The Understanding

The basic interpretation for this period comes from the writer of the Deuteronomic history. This writer presented the theological history of Israel from Joshua to Kings. The author's basic evaluation is found in chapter 2 of Judges. The following are the basic elements: (1) God brought them out of Egypt into the land which he had promised; (2) although God had kept his covenant, Israel, which had been commanded to refrain from making covenants, disobeyed God and persisted in making covenants with foreign gods; (3) as a result of Israel's infidelity, God would not protect them from the adversaries but would allow them to become snares to them. Therefore, we have the theme of sin, punishment, and deliverance in the stories of the Judges.

Disobedience to God was the key element in the biblical writer's understanding of Israel's experience. Therefore, the author of Judges attributes the Israelites' constant struggles to their going after false gods. The experience of the period of Gideon is illustrative of his view:

> As soon as Gideon died, the people of Israel turned again and played the harlot after the Baals, and made Baalberith their god. And the people of Israel did not remember the Lord their God, who had rescued them from the hand of all their enemies on every side; and they did not show kindness to the family of Jerubbaal (that is, Gideon) in return for all the good that he had done to Israel (Judges 8:33-35).

This is one of the recurring problems which disturbed the relationship between God and the Chosen People. Georg Fohrer has characterized this period as one of conflict between Yahwism (the worship of Israel's God) and the Canaanite religion.[3] The biblical narratives reflect this same understanding and Israel's God stood in opposition to other gods who were real powers (cf. Judges 11:21f.). Israel's worship at the shrine of any of these other gods was the cause for God's wrath. Israel's punishment was invasion by the neighboring nations.

THE CROSSING POINT

The crossing point for the relationship between the periods of the conquest and settlement and our life today has been put into sharp focus by the theological interpretation of the Deuteronomist. What is the relationship between verbal assent, ritual practice, and true commitment? Is it enough to shout, "We will serve God," and perform pious rituals without the integrity to follow through on what this means?

The Deuteronomist made it clear that Israel failed in her commitment. He reminded her of her sin. This biblical writer speaks to us today. We have the form of religion but deny the power thereof. We cry, "Lord, Lord," but do not commit ourselves to the things God demands of us. Our only response can be: "It's me, it's me, O Lord, standing in the need of prayer. It's me, it's me, O Lord, standing in the need of prayer." Yet the biblical writer indicated that God was forgiving. God was not an arbitrary sultan who changed his promises willy-nilly. He was still faithful. Israel might renege on her promises, but God remained faithful.

This was the message that the writer was conveying. God is true and faithful. If Israel would return, he would forgive. The record of the conquest and settlement illustrated that whenever the people of Israel returned to God, he was willing to forgive them.

The belief in God as one who forgives when we return to him is the same theme that was treated in the story of the creation, only this time instead of Adam's sin we have Israel's sin. This belief in God's forgiveness is the heart of the gospel—this is the Good News. The period of conquest and settlement is a mirror of our rebellion, but at the same time it is a reminder that in returning to God we find forgiveness.

Israel's willful disobedience to God and her seeking to establish relationship with foreign gods is illustrated in the New Testament parable of the prodigal son. Although the son was in the security of his father's house, he sought a new way and ended in the pigpen. His rejection of his father's house is suggestive of Israel's rejection of God. It is suggestive, too, of how we sometimes seek the wrong way to freedom.

As we explore the story of the prodigal son, we are aware that he chose the wrong way to freedom. As we observe the prodigal son, we discover that his concept of freedom was his independence from his father's home. His destination was to seek only himself and his own free development. He acted upon the assumption that if he remained within the confining tradition and value structure of his father's home, he would not be able to find himself in freedom, but that he would remain in bondage and unfree. So he separated himself from his father and took his journey to the far country.

But the story does not end there. The son returned. There was acceptance; there was joy; there was celebration. This is the message for those of us who, like Israel and the young man, make wrong decisions. The way to freedom and fulfillment is acceptance of the father's love!

QUESTIONS FOR FURTHER CONSIDERATION

• How is the sovereignty of God related to the concept of democracy and the value of personal freedom?

• How are we as Christians to acknowledge God's sovereignty?

• What are the roles of inward knowing, prayer, and meditation in acknowledging God's sovereignty?

• How do we as Christians resolve the tension between self-surrender and self-love?

• Are euthanasia and abortion options for Christians who believe in the sovereignty of God? Why or why not?

The Rise
of the Monarchy:
The Trials
and Tribulations of a
Developing Nation
Chapter 6

The United States recently celebrated the 200th anniversary of the signing of the Declaration of Independence. This was a significant event in the nation's history. Yet the real significance of this event was what the colonies did following the signing. This has been called the American Experiment. The significance of this is conveyed to one who visits the Hall of Presidents at Disney World in Florida. This is a brilliant presentation of the founding of the country and the role of the presidents through the years. It highlights the kind of democracy which emerged out of the Declaration of Independence and other documents—a democracy that for the first time attempted to establish a government "of the people, by the people, and for the people." We know that these goals have not at some points been fulfilled; nevertheless the goals remain. Likewise, the monarchy of Israel emerged with noble goals—a holy people, a holy city, a holy temple, a holy monarchy—all given to God. The worship practices were to manifest these goals, but somehow the goals were forgotten in the rush of events. There were many experiences that were significant in Israel's life during this critical period in their history. The account is vividly chronicled in First and Second Samuel. The principal characters are Samuel, Saul, and David.

THE EXPERIENCE

The settlement in Canaan provided the Israelites with many opportunities but also difficult problems. One could call this period "trials and tribulations of a developing nation." This period began with the story of Samuel and ended with the last days of Solomon's reign. The three kings during that time were Saul, David, and Solomon. Samuel, the last of the judges, was instrumental in the rise of the first two kings, David and Saul, to the throne of Israel.

By way of background, let us look at the role of Samuel. His career is described in 1 Samuel 1:1–7:17. He is presented as a judge, but basically he was more of an administrator than a judge, with characteristics of a charismatic leader. In response to the decadent life of Eli's son and the general state of despair in Israel, Samuel sought to fill the void of a leaderless people. This despair is largely pictured through Eli's daughter-in-law who named her son Ichabod:

> And she named the child Ichabod, saying, "The glory has departed from Israel!" because the ark of God had been captured and because of her father-in-law and her husband. And she said, "The glory has departed from Israel, for the ark of God has been captured" (1 Samuel 4:21-22).

Samuel's life had a pattern similar to that of Moses and Samson. He was a child of his parents' late age. Like Sarah, his mother Hannah felt that she could have no children. However, she prayed for children, and Samuel was born in answer to her prayer (1 Samuel 1:9-20). As an act of gratitude Hannah dedicated Samuel to God and sent the young boy to the house of Eli, the priest (1 Samuel 1:21-28), where he received a call (3:2-14). Samuel's primary function was to lead Israel away from apostasy and to restore fidelity to God (1 Samuel 7:3-17).

Samuel's most significant role was as a kingmaker. He anointed both Saul and David as kings of Israel. Saul was the first king anointed by Samuel.

Saul

There are two varying accounts that treat Saul's ascendancy to the kingship. In the first account the Israelites asked for a king (1 Samuel 8:1-22). There seemed to be two reasons for this request. First, they wanted to emulate the surrounding nations. Secondly, and more significantly, they desired stronger leadership to cope with the constant threats from the surrounding nations:

> Then all the elders of Israel gathered together and came to Samuel at Ramah, and said to him, "Behold, you are old and your sons do not walk in your ways; now appoint for us a king to govern us like all the nations." But the thing displeased Samuel when they

said, "Give us a king to govern us." And Samuel prayed to the Lord
(1 Samuel 8:4-6).

In this first account the author of Samuel sees the request for a king
as a rejection of God:

> And the Lord said to Samuel, "Hearken to the voice of the people
> in all that they say to you; for they have not rejected you, but they
> have rejected me from being king over them" (1 Samuel 8:7; cf. 1
> Samuel 10:17-27).

In the second account, the selection of a king is seen as God's choice
for deliverance from the Philistines (1Samuel 9:1–10:16). From this
perspective, Samuel's role as seer provided the context for the
meeting of Samuel with Saul—through divine revelation he
identified Saul as the designated leader:

> Now the day before Saul came, the Lord had revealed to Samuel:
> "Tomorrow about this time I will send to you a man from the land
> of Benjamin, and you shall anoint him to be prince over my people
> Israel. He shall save my people from the hand of the Philistines; for
> I have seen the affliction of my people, because their cry has come
> to me." When Samuel saw Saul, the Lord told him, "Here is the
> man of whom I spoke to you! He it is who shall rule over my
> people" (1 Samuel 9:15-17).

These two accounts reflect two different views of the beginning of
the monarchy. Both were apparently common views in Israel.

From either perspective of his selection, Saul began his career as a
military hero, having won a smashing victory against the Ammonites
before he was acclaimed king at Gilgal. He continued this military
feat with victory over the Philistines at the pass of Michmash, thanks
to the daring courage of his son Jonathan (1 Samuel 14:1-31). He was
constantly at war (1 Samuel 14:47, 52).

His external warfare was accompanied by conflicts with Samuel
and David, and eventually this led to his rejection by both of them.
The first conflict between Samuel and Saul emerged when Saul
assumed the special right of Samuel and offered sacrifices on the eve
of a battle against the Philistines when Samuel was late in arriving (1
Samuel 13:8-14). The second conflict emerged when Saul refused to
follow the practice of *herem*—total destruction of the enemy and

conquered goods (cf. Numbers 21:2-4; Deuteronomy 20:10-18; Joshua 6:17, 21). Following a battle with the Amalakites, Samuel rebuked Saul in a well-known passage which stresses the difference between sacrifice and obedience:

And Samuel said,
"Has the Lord as great delight in burnt offerings and sacrifices,
    as in obeying the voice of the Lord?
Behold, to obey is better than sacrifice,
    and to hearken than the fat of rams.
For rebellion is as the sin of divination,
    and stubbornness is as iniquity and idolatry.
Because you have rejected the word of the Lord,
    he has also rejected you from being king."
                                        —1 Samuel 15:22-24

In addition to Saul's conflict with Samuel, Saul also had difficulty with David who had been introduced to his court as a musician (1 Samuel 16:14-23). However, it seems from what followed that Saul's jealousy of David was due to his exploits as a warrior. David gained fame as the victorious leader of many battles. Probably his most famous victory was his slaying of Goliath, the Philistine giant (1 Samuel 17–18:1-5). As a result, women, in David's praise, sang: "Saul has slain his thousands, and David his ten thousands" (1 Samuel 18:7*b*).

Saul's jealousy intensified and drove him to make several abortive attempts to kill David (1 Samuel 19:9-17; 20:12-42), but David was saved by his friend Jonathan, the son of Saul. David fled to the wilderness, forced to become an outlaw (1 Samuel 22:1-23). This conflict between David and Saul lasted three or four years until Saul was killed in battle at the fort of Mount Gilboa (1 Samuel 28). Saul's death left Israel leaderless. Into such a void David came to power.

David

David was first crowned king of Judah and later was also crowned king of Israel. He came to power at a time when Israel was in a precarious state following the death of Saul. Israel felt vulnerable to the Philistines since Israel did not have a strong king. The surviving son of Saul, Ishbosheth, had been made king at Mahanaim with the support of Abner, Saul's commander-in-chief, and other leaders loyal to Saul (2 Samuel 2:8f.). This action did not include Judah since David had already been selected to replace Saul as king of Judah (2 Samuel 2:1-4). Later Abner and Ishbosheth broke relations as a result of accusations that Abner was involved with one of Saul's concubines; a relationship with a concubine was a sign that one had desire for political control. Therefore, Abner withdrew his support from Ishbosheth and committed himself to David as king (2 Samuel 3:6-12). But Joab, David's strong man, slew Abner (2 Samuel 3:26-30), and Ishbosheth died a brutal death (2 Samuel 4). This series of events paved the way for the tribes, which until now had remained loyal to the house of Saul, to accept David as king of all of Israel:

> Then all the tribes of Israel came to David at Hebron, and said, "Behold, we are your bone and flesh. In times past, when Saul was king over us, it was you that led out and brought in Israel; and the Lord said to you, 'You shall be shepherd of my people Israel, and you shall be prince over Israel.'" So all the elders of Israel came to the king at Hebron; and King David made a covenant with them at Hebron before the Lord, and they anointed David king over Israel (2 Samuel 5:1-3; cf. 1 Chronicles 11:1-9).

Consolidation of the Kingdom

This event projected David to a unique place in Israel's history. He was the charismatic leader and established ruler. David's rise to power combined the role of the charismatic leader (*nagid*) and the king (*melek*). David's kingship continued both of the traditions of leadership; yet at the same time the structure of David's kingship marked a departure from earlier Israelite political organization. The power before this time was in the tribal league. Whatever unity existed was due to the loose confederation tied around the allegiance to God and concretized by the covenant relationship and cultic observances. But when David, who had already assumed kingship of the tribes in the south, united under his leadership the northern tribes that had been under the loyalty to the house of Saul, the unifying factor became the person of David himself. This in itself is a significant change.

The union effected by David was constantly on the brink of collapsing. It was, to say the least, a brittle union. However, David

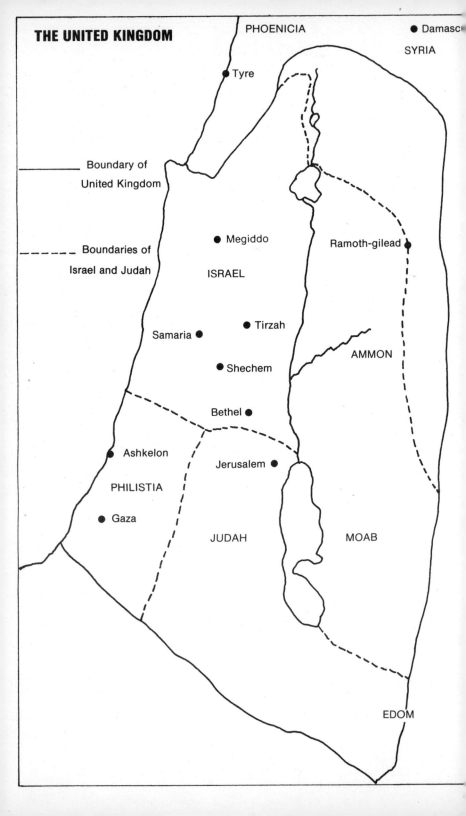

proceeded with the task of solidifying the state. He was finally able to subdue the Philistines (2 Samuel 5:17-25; cf. 1 Chronicles 14:8-16). He also established a new capital at Jerusalem (2 Samuel 5:6-10) and transferred the ark of the covenant there (2 Samuel 6:1-23; cf. 1 Chronicles 13:1–16:43). David also appointed Abiathar and Zadok high priests. All of these were strategies by David to combine the religious and political dimensions at one place (2 Samuel 7). Having solidified his internal organization, religiously and politically, he began the task of expanding his empire (2 Samuel 8:1-18; cf. 1 Chronicles 18:1-7).

The conquest of the Moabites and Edomites in the Southern Transjordan (2 Samuel 8:2, 13) was a part of this strategy. David also conducted campaigns in Syria which were also successful. This was a great time for this emerging power:

> So David reigned over all Israel; and David administered justice and equity to all his people. And Joab the son of Zeruiah was over the army; and Jehoshaphat the son of Ahilud was recorder; and Zadok the son of Ahitub and Ahimelech the son of Abiathar were priests; and Seraiah was secretary; and Benaiah the son of Jehoiada was over the Cherethites and the Pelethites; and David's sons were priests (2 Samuel 8:15-18; cf. 1 Chronicles 18:14-17).

Having successfully consolidated and expanded his empire, David proceeded to organize the expanding territories. Israel now included Palestine and the surrounding areas. It was no longer a tribal confederacy but a complex empire. (See the map of the United Kingdom.)

Internal Problems

David reigned for many years following his conquests. He maintained control of the boundaries which he had conquered but suffered from internal struggles at home. David's domestic situation was in constant turmoil. One source of trouble came from his son Absalom who rebelled against him (2 Samuel 13:1–18:33). This revolt by his son was precipitated by Amnon's rape of Tamar, his half-sister, who was Absalom's sister. In revenge Absalom slew Amnon, after waiting two years for David to take some action against Amnon (2 Samuel 13:1-38). Absalom became a fugitive, but after five years he was able to return as a result of Joab's intercession with David (2 Samuel 14:1-33).

When Absalom returned, he began to plot to seize the throne (2 Samuel 15:1-12). After four years he went to Hebron and anointed himself king. David did not expect this move and had to flee the city (2 Samuel 15:13-29). This attack was nothing more than an outburst of Absalom and a few of David's enemies. As a result David was able to rally his forces under Joab's leadership and put down the revolt. In the struggle Absalom was slain (2 Samuel 18:1-15). In deep remorse David mourned, saying, "O my son Absalom, my son, my son Absalom! Would I had died instead of you . . ." (2 Samuel 18:33).

Absalom's attack upon his father was followed by another revolt from a different element in the kingdom. This time there was dissatisfaction from the northern tribes. They were angry because David did not keep his promise to select Amasa to replace Joab who had killed Absalom in open defiance of David's orders. They considered David's retention of Joab as an example of favoritism. As a result the northern tribes attempted to withdraw from Judah. The leader of this revolt was Sheba, the Benjaminite (2 Samuel 20:1-26). David, with Joab, quickly ended the revolt, and David's throne remained secure.

On the basis of this discussion we can see that in spite of David's great leadership in expanding the empire, he was unsuccessful in preventing serious internal problems. In addition to the rebellions by Absalom and Sheba, he was confronted by two problems which related to succession to the throne. One had to do with the rivalry between the house of Saul and the house of David, and the other related to the rivalry between David's two sons.

The first aspect of the problem of succession grew out of the rivalry between the house of David and the house of Saul. David's succession did not solve this problem. Neither did his marriage to Saul's daughter, Michal, resolve the problem since they separated before any children were born (2 Samuel 6:20-23). The only descendant of Saul was Mephibosheth, who was the lame son of Jonathan. Although David made him a pensioner in his court, the followers of Saul were hesitant to acquiesce to the principle of dynastic succession.

In addition to the problem of the followers of Saul was the jealousy of David's remaining sons who, by the time of David's old age, had been reduced to two. Adonijah was David's oldest living son (2 Samuel 3:4), and Solomon was the son of Bathsheba, the widow of Uriah. David had seduced Bathsheba and had her husband put on the front line of battle to die. As a result of this he had been denounced by Nathan, the prophet (2 Samuel 12:9-12). Both Solomon and Adonijah had supporters within David's court. Adonijah was supported in his claim to the throne by Joab and Abiathar, the priest. Solomon was supported by Nathan, the prophet; Zadok, the priest; and Benaiah, the leader of David's foreign mercenaries. The intrigue and drama are described in classic details in the first two chapters of First Kings. First, Adonijah sought to make himself king:

> Now Adonijah the son of Haggith exalted himself, saying, "I will be king"; and he prepared for himself chariots and horsemen, and fifty men to run before him. His father had never at any time displeased him by asking, "Why have you done thus and so?" He was also a very handsome man; and he was born next after Absalom. He conferred with Joab the son of Zeruiah and with Abiathar the priest; and they followed Adonijah and helped him. But Zadok the priest, and Benaiah the son of Jehoiada, and Nathan the prophet, and Shimei, and Rei, and David's mighty men were not with Adonijah. Adonijah sacrificed sheep, oxen, and fatlings by the Serpent's Stone, which is beside Enrogel, and he invited all his brothers, the king's sons, and all the royal officials of Judah, but he did not invite Nathan the prophet or Benaiah or the mighty men or Solomon his brother (1 Kings 1:5-10).

While he was attempting to do this, the prophet Nathan, Bathsheba (Solomon's mother), Zadok (the priest), and Solomon told David what Adonijah was doing and thereby gained David's permission to anoint Solomon king at Gihon (1 Kings 1:32-40). Thus Solomon became king and succeeded his father as ruler of Israel. To secure his reign, Solomon killed Adonijah, Joab, and Shimei, a relative of Saul's (2 Samuel 16:5-8), and expelled Abiathar, the priest who supported Absalom, from Jerusalem to Anathoth, his homeland (1 Kings 2:13-46). Then he proceeded to the task of maintaining his father's empire: ". . . the kingdom was established in the hand of Solomon" (1 Kings 2:46). He began a new era in Israel's "golden age."

Solomon

Solomon is described as providing for a new day in Israel's cultural, social, and economic growth. He was what the ancient Near East would call a "wise man." The biblical account depicts Solomon as sage, builder, and international prince.

Solomon the Sage

The intent of these first texts that deal with Solomon's reign is to show that Solomon was a "wise man." To be "wise" was not so much to serve the great concept of Wisdom, to be master of intellect or abstract truth. Rather, the wise man in the ancient Near East was the person who was successful in life, arts, and politics. Two stories illustrate this meaning of "wisdom" in the Old Testament (1 Kings 3:16-28; 10:1-13). These stories are written to illustrate that Solomon ruled as a wise king. He was also a successful administrator (chapter 4), builder (chapters 5–7), and trader (chapters 9–10). Thus, the writer concludes:

> And God gave Solomon wisdom and understanding beyond measure, and largeness of mind like the sand on the seashore, so that Solomon's wisdom surpassed the wisdom of all the people of the east, and all the wisdom of Egypt (1 Kings 4:29).

Solomon the Builder

The role of Solomon as builder focuses upon his two significant accomplishments—the temple and the palace. His first project was the building of the temple. He selected Hiram of Tyre as architect and builder (1 Kings 7:13f.). The Temple of Solomon does not compare with elegant cathedrals which were built in the Middle Ages, such as Salisbury in England or the Notre Dame in Paris. Nevertheless, it was a great feat in his day. It included a vestibule; a main hall of the sanctuary of the Holy Place; a large, rectangular chamber with small windows under the roof; and a small, windowless cube which contained the ark of the covenant. The construction of the building began in Solomon's fourth year and was completed seven years later with a great ceremony of dedication (1 Kings 8:12-21). His dedicatory prayer is a classic statement of Israel's faith:

> Then Solomon stood before the altar of the Lord in the presence

of all the assembly of Israel, and spread forth his hands toward heaven; and said, "O Lord, God of Israel, there is no God like thee, in heaven above or on earth beneath, keeping covenant and showing steadfast love to thy servants who walk before thee with all their heart; who hast kept with thy servant David my father what thou didst declare to him; yea, thou didst speak with thy mouth, and with thy hand hast fulfilled it this day. Now therefore, O Lord, God of Israel, keep with thy servant David my father what thou hast promised him, saying, 'There shall never fail you a man before me to sit upon the throne of Israel, if only your sons take heed to their way, to walk before me as you have walked before me.' Now therefore, O God of Israel, let thy word be confirmed, which thou hast spoken to thy servant David my father" (1 Kings 8:22-26).

The temple served a two-fold purpose. It was to be a royal chapel where the priests appointed by the king officiated. Also it was to be a national shrine where the people gathered for the national festivities.

The second great building program was the palace (1 Kings 7:1-8). It was called the "House of the Forest of Lebanon" because of the great pillars that supported it. It included a judgment hall in which there was an ivory throne. (This was the area where the business of state was conducted.)

Solomon as International Prince

The third focus of Solomon's reign was upon his role as international prince. Solomon sought to maintain the amicable relationship which his father David had established with the surrounding nations. His strategy was to enter into an alliance with these vassals and allies. Many of these alliances were consummated by marriage to the daughters of the reigning monarchs (1 Kings 11:3). Included among them was the daughter of Pharaoh for whom he built a special room in the palace. He was also able to negotiate an alliance with Tyre (1 Kings 5:1-12). These alliances became a basis for his trade agreements.

The primary reference for Solomon's fame as an international prince was his ability to develop a trade relationship with the countries along the Red Sea. He successfully conducted the caravan trade through his relationship with the Queen of Sheba (1 Kings 10:1-

10). Solomon also developed the gold and silver (1 Kings 10:11-22) industries in addition to trade in horses and chariots (1 Kings 10:26-29). These ventures caused Solomon's fame to spread:

> Thus King Solomon excelled all the kings of the earth in riches and in wisdom. And the whole earth sought the presence of Solomon to hear his wisdom, which God had put into his mind. Every one of them brought his present, articles of silver and gold, garments, myrrh, spices, horses, and mules, so much year by year (1 Kings 10:23-25).

This comment on the reign of Solomon is similar to many such editorials in the books of Kings which help us to get the feeling that we are there during the reigns of Saul, Solomon, and David.

THE UNDERSTANDING

Recently I attended a theater that housed a 360-degree giant screen in which I could see the picture from any angle. I could see in front, on the sides, and behind me—all at the same time. This is the kind of feeling that one gets as the story of the period of the monarchy is told. One feels the contemporaneity of the events. Although the events took place in a linear fashion, the theme of God's lordship and his demands for Israel's loyalty are pictured all around us. Unlike the previous periods studied, some of the accounts were written during the same time that the events were described. Just as the old television program "You Are There" sought to give the viewer the feeling of a front-seat view of past events, so the writers of First and Second Samuel and First and Second Kings create for us the same feeling as they share experiences and understanding of the Israelites during the period of the monarchy.

The period of the monarchy is the keystone of Israel's history. The records bear witness to this. In addition to the biblical texts, archaeological discoveries and contemporary texts from other ancient Near Eastern countries which surrounded the Israelites help us to understand this period. They help us to understand some of the ambiguities in the biblical accounts. One such problem are the two versions of the election of Saul. These two versions (1 Samuel 8; 10:17-27; 12; and 9:1–10:16; 11) reveal the mixed understanding of the role of the monarchy. Yehezkel Kaufmann, the renowned Jewish scholar, states: "Both versions of Saul's election are correct. . . . A king was desperately needed; would YHWH [Yahweh] ignore this need? Samuel's activity is, therefore, divided; he opposes a king, but he is the one who in the end anoints Saul in the name of YHWH."[1] This is the double view of kingship, and it is integral to the basic understanding that the Israelites had of the monarchy. Although the kingship was a different type of divine instrument from the temporary charismatic leader, God was still responding to their needs. This is the understanding that the Israelites had. The king was evidence of God's divine activity in Israel. At the same time emphasis was put upon the dangers of the kingship.

The awareness of Israel's understanding of God's continual care helps us to see why the kings of the united monarchy were described as possessing the Spirit of God (1 Samuel 19:23f.; 2 Samuel 23:2). Also, Solomon was a wise man possessed by the wisdom (spirit) of God:

> and all Israel heard of the judgment which the king had rendered; and they stood in awe of the king, because they perceived that the wisdom of God was in him, to render justice (1 Kings 3:28).

The kingship of these men was understood as a manifestation of God's kingship. God was king. He anointed Saul, David, and Solomon to lead his people. The same God who had delivered the Israelites from bondage in Egypt, who had brought them into the Promised Land, and who had raised up judges to overcome their enemy had designated "his anointed" to rule over his people (1 Samuel 10:24; 16:1ff.; 2 Samuel 6:21; Deuteronomy 17:15). This understanding of the kingship is seen in the theological legitimization that David and Solomon gave to the monarchy by the transfer of the Ark of the Covenant to Jerusalem and the erection of the temple as a permanent place for God to dwell.

The ark was the symbol of unity for the northern and southern tribes. David's role in bringing the ark to Jerusalem was symbolic of his role as a sacred person.

Solomon followed in the footsteps of his father. Just as his father David had made the movement of the ark to Jerusalem the key to his reign, Solomon distinguished himself by the erection of the temple (1 Kings 8:1-66).

Another aspect of the understanding of the experience of the period of the monarchy was Israel's idolatry or what Kaufmann refers to as Israel's second "idolatrous period." In spite of Solomon's reputation as the wise prince, builder, administrator, and international leader, his reign was also divided into two parts. On the one hand, the writers of the biblical text viewed the major part of his reign as successful, but because of Solomon's religious policies the last part was seen as evil and idolatrous. One of the themes introduced here and developed in the next period by the prophets was Israel's turning away from the covenant and their adoption of idolatrous practices. Idolatry was unfaithfulness to God's covenant.

THE CROSSING POINT

The period of the monarchy reminds us of the fallacy of dependence upon human institutions and human prowess. The writers of the biblical narratives constantly emphasize that faith and commitment belong to God and to him alone. Any human instrumentality must be viewed as subservient to God's demands upon our lives. The theologian Schleiermacher echoed this theme many years ago when he defined religion as the absolute dependence upon God. This is the message we receive from the monarchy. This message is illustrated in the critical judgment which the writers made of the kings, especially in reference to their human weaknesses. Saul was given to ravenous jealousy; David was given to predatory lust; and Solomon was given to spiritual infidelity. Although the monarchy offered a great potential in the hands of these leaders, it became the root of Israel's falling away from God.

Henri J. M. Nouwen, in his recent book *The Wounded Healer,* relates a story from ancient India which is suggestive for us today as we discuss the crossing point between the period of the monarchy and Christian faith. Four sons were seeking to determine what their specialty should be. Each agreed to search the earth and develop mastery in a certain science. They also agreed to meet at an appointed place and time to report on their findings. After a while they returned and reported their discoveries. The first reported that he had developed a method to create flesh on a bone. The second reported that he knew how to grow skin and hair if the creature had flesh on its bone. The third reported that he could create limbs if he had flesh, skin, and hair. The fourth added that he could give life to that creature if its form was complete with limbs.

Having shared their specialties, they went into the jungle to look for a bone to demonstrate their mastery of the special sciences. They found a bone but unfortunately did not know it was a lion's bone; so the one with the ability to grow flesh on the bone added flesh. The second demonstrated his ability to grow hide and hair; and the third made matching limbs, after which the fourth gave life to the lion. Immediately the lion arose and killed the sons who had created him and went away.[2]

This story illustrates the period of the monarchy. Israel wanted a king, and the infidelity of the kings led Israel astray. The kings, who were supposed to be servants of God to lead Israel in worshiping God in the temple and in keeping the covenant, turned on Israel. They went after foreign gods and fell into immoral ways. Over and over again the kings put more emphasis upon their power and might and rejected God.

Today we manifest this same tendency to put our faith in human powers and human instrumentalities. We want to be our own master and forget about God. Israel's life during the monarchy reminds us that human rulers and leaders are human creatures and are subject to human weakness. Thus worship of any human being is idolatry. God requires ultimate loyalty!

QUESTIONS FOR FURTHER CONSIDERATION

• What do the experiences of Israel in the period of the monarchy say to us as we seek leadership for our own nation?

• Are our expectations that the president should be a person with vision valid?

• Have we been bestowing upon the presidency almost monarchical powers? How much have we looked to the president for the solution to our problems, rather than each of us taking responsibility for creating a moral climate on the one hand and doing some thoughtful intellectual work about economic solutions, fair pricing, concern for the welfare system, the hungry, and the like?

The Divided Kingdom: The Experience

Chapter 7

John Philpot Curran, a politician, in a speech on the election of the Lord Mayor of Dublin, July 10, 1790, wrote: "The condition upon which God hath given liberty to man is eternal vigilance; which condition if he break, servitude is at once the consequence of his crime, and the punishment of his guilt."[1] This statement is helpful for placing in perspective the experiences of the Hebrews during the period of the monarchy. This period forces us to examine the meaning of liberty and the nature of responsible nationhood. At the height of Israel's supremacy, the meaning of eternal vigilance was lost.

The period from the death of Solomon in 922 B.C. to the fall of the Southern Kingdom in 586 B.C. was characterized by successes and failures. At times there were periods of peace and satisfaction, but at many times there was confusion and frustration. It marked the transition from Israel's existence as a splendid empire under the reigns of David and Solomon to the subjugation of the divided kingdoms under Assyrian domination. It was a time when the solidity of the Davidic empire was divided and subsequently destroyed. (Because of the large amount of material to be covered, this chapter will deal only with the experience of the divided kingdom. The discussion of the understanding and crossing point will be found in the next chapter.)

The outline of this period is provided by the synoptic history of the kings of Israel and Judah in 1 Kings 12:1 through 2 Kings 16:20. It begins with the story of the division of the kingdoms when Rehoboam, after having angered the elders at Shechem, was accepted as king only by the house of Judah (1 Kings 12:21).

Martin Noth, widely acclaimed biblical scholar, in his classic work

The History of Israel has noted that the division of the kingdom was rooted in two views of the nature of the succession to the monarchy. His insight provides the perspective for understanding Rehoboam's abortive reply and the elders' radical response.

We have noted earlier that the selection of David to succeed Saul was not based upon his kinship with Saul. David possessed the characteristics of the charismatic leaders who appeared during the period of the judges. This style of leadership was seen as evidence of the divine call. David became king because God anointed him and bestowed his "spiritual" gift, "charisma," upon him. The ambiguities surrounding Solomon's succession left this issue still unresolved. Solomon's succession was more the result of the coup d'etat (a forced takeover of power) rather than an orderly succession to power by virtue of his being an heir of David. The noted biblical scholar, R. N. Whybray, has treated this theme in his study of the succession narrative in 2 Samuel 9–20 and 1 Kings 1 and 2.

The key part of this study for our purposes is 2 Samuel 13–19. Whybray contends that these chapters were written to show how it was that Solomon became the legitimate successor to his father David. In other words, these chapters are a defense of Solomon's kingship. In reference to the succession narrative Whybray writes:

> . . . the Succession Narrative was written during the early years of Solomon's reign, soon after the events described in I Kings 2, and while the régime was still threatened by disaffected parties: it is primarily a political document intended to support the régime by demonstrating its legitimacy and justifying its policies. 2

This tension that revolved around Solomon's right to sonship was somewhat reduced because of his successful reign. However, near the end of his reign dissatisfaction with him and his policies forecast trouble.

THE KINGDOM DIVIDES

After Solomon's death, the elders who met with Rehoboam at Shechem were not convinced that the kingship automatically belonged to the heir of Solomon; they would accept him as king, but only upon his fulfillment of their expectations. Rehoboam, Solomon's son, assumed that the kingship was automatically his, and thus he responded to the request for relief from the heavy taxation and oppressive policies of his father with arrogance and hardness of heart. Immediately dissension arose, and Jeroboam, who had been exiled by Solomon, led the northern tribes in revolt. This precipitous event marked the beginning of the divided kingdoms. In order to prevent further loss of power, Rehoboam gathered with the members of the house of Judah and the tribe of Benjamin, and 180,000 chosen warriors, and had himself proclaimed king at Jerusalem (1 Kings 12:21-24). David's kingdom which once symbolized the unity of Israel was now reduced in size to a small part of the territory that was previously occupied under united Israel.

The unsolved problem of succession was manifested in the nature of two kingships which emerged from this critical moment in Israel's history. In Judah, the Southern Kingdom, the Davidic dynasty prevailed; although there were times of trouble, Rehoboam and his heirs remained in power. In contrast, the followers to the throne in Israel, the Northern Kingdom, were subject to usurpation by ambitious charismatic leaders. Finally, Israel shifted to a more stable monarchy as the system of charismatic leaders in Israel's history proved unworkable. This contrast had several distinct periods.

The experience of the Israelites during this period can be interpreted from the phrase "from order to chaos." The social, economic, cultural, political, and religious life of the people was affected by the division between the kingdoms. Instead of a unified thrust, they were divided one against another. The social experience was predicated by the two types of societies in which they lived. The Northern Kingdom had more contact with other nations, while the Southern Kingdom was more isolated. These social settings resulted in different life-styles and different attitudes. Their economic styles were also different. The economy was based upon commercial contacts and a diversified economy in the Northern Kingdom. Judah's economy, on the other hand, was based on an agricultural and pastoral basis.

The different social and economic milieus provided for a different cultural expression. The northern cultural expression reflected the influence of the surrounding nations, an assimilation with countries like Phoenicia and Syria. Judah, on the other hand, had a cultural expression which was more closely related to the earlier life of Israel when she first arrived in Canaan. It was more primitive and agricultural.

The political history falls in two distinct periods—the existence of the two kingdoms north and south (1 Kings 12—2 Kings 18:12) from the death of Solomon in 922 B.C. to 722 B.C., and the existence of the Southern Kingdom (2 Kings 18:13-25:26) from the end of the Northern Kingdom to the destruction of the Southern Kingdom in 587 B.C. Much activity is described in the biblical texts, but for our purposes we will only review the basic historical development as recorded in the Bible.

THE AFTERMATH OF THE SCHISM

This division began with the parallel reigns of Jeroboam, 922–915 B.C., in the Northern Kingdom, Israel, (1 Kings 12:1-33); and Rehoboam, 922–901 B.C., in the Southern Kingdom, Judah, (1 Kings 14:21-31).

When Rehoboam came to Jerusalem, he assembled all the house of Judah, and the tribe of Benjamin, a hundred and eighty thousand chosen warriors, to fight against the house of Israel, to restore the kingdom of Rehoboam the son of Solomon. But the word of God came to Shemaiah the man of God: "Say to Rehoboam the son of Solomon, king of Judah, and to all the house of Judah and Benjamin, and to the rest of the people, 'Thus says the Lord, You shall not go up or fight against your kinsmen the people of Israel. Return every man to his home, for this thing is for me.'" So they hearkened to the word of the Lord, and went home again, according to the word of the Lord (1 Kings 12:21-24).

During this period, Israel, under Jeroboam, worshiped at Bethel, and Jeroboam moved the administrative center from Penuel, near Shechem the capital, to Tirzah. Judah kept Jerusalem as the capital city and the center of worship. These were only symbols of the great schisms which were developing. Following Rehoboam and Jeroboam their successors continued the hostility between the two rival kingdoms. The first fifty years of the divided kingdoms were characterized by sporadic sectional warfare between Judah and Israel. Both were weakened by this deadly warfare.

Judah at this time was relatively stable under the reigns of Abijam

(915–913 B.C.: 1 Kings 15:1-8) and Asa (913–873 B.C.: 1 Kings 15:9-24) while Israel experienced political assassinations and chaos. A succession of leaders assumed the throne: Nadab (901–900 B.C.: 1 Kings 15:25-31), Baasha (900–877 B.C.: 1 Kings 15:33–16:7), Elah (877–876 B.C.: 1 Kings 16:8-14), Zimri (876 B.C. (one week): 1 Kings 16:15-20), and Omri (1 Kings 16:23-28). One can observe from this long list of kings that evil was the order of the day. Omri was able to bring peace to this troubled kingdom.

The Dynasty of Omri (876–842 B.C.)

Omri is given a negative evaluation by the chronicler:

> Omri did what was evil in the sight of the Lord, and he did more evil than all who were before him. For he walked in all the way of Jeroboam the son of Nebat, and in the sins which he made Israel to sin, provoking the Lord, the God of Israel, to anger by their idols. Now the rest of the acts of Omri which he did, and the might that he showed, are they not written in the Book of the Chronicles of the Kings of Israel? And Omri slept with his fathers, and was buried in Samaria; and Ahab his son reigned in his stead (1 Kings 16:25-28).

Although Omri is not given a good report, one can infer from the text that his career was not devoid of political achievement. Archaeological discoveries indicate that Omri relocated Israel's capital from Tirzah to Samaria (1 Kings 16:24). His palace was also noted for its ivory (1 Kings 22:39); and he also improved Israel's defense.

Omri was the father of Ahab (869–850 B.C.), the king who was confronted by Elijah. We shall return to this later. Omri gave his son in marriage to another notorious biblical character, Jezebel, the daughter of Ethbaal (Ithbaal) the king of Phoenicia. This marriage, like many marriages during that time, was political in nature and was an attempt by Omri to strengthen his alliance with the king of Phoenicia. Omri was responsible for expanding the borders of Israel. Some suggest that in comparison with the other kings of the Northern Kingdom, Omri was referred to as the David of Israel. This was primarily a military connotation and does not relate to any other aspect of David's reign.

Omri's successor was his son Ahab (869–850 B.C.). Ahab is

presented in the Bible as the precipitator of a religious crisis in Israel. Nevertheless, he was successful in repelling the Syrian attack on at least two occasions (1 Kings 20:1-21, 23-34).

This victory over the Syrians provided the basis for Israel to form an alliance with Syria against Shalmaneser III of Syria (855–824 B.C.). Subsequently, the hostility between the two countries emerged again, and Ahab joined with Jehoshaphat of Judah in an attempt to reclaim the Syrian-held Ramoth-gilead. Ahab was killed in battle (1 Kings 22:1-40). Ahab's reign is given an extensive treatment because his political and religious policies brought him into conflict with Israel's religious commitment to God. Elijah, the Tishbite, was God's spokesman to Ahab.

The confrontation between Elijah and Ahab is illustrative of the conflict between Israel and apostasy, their abandonment of God. We shall discuss the role of the prophet during our treatment in the next chapter of the understanding Israel had of this period. We introduce this matter at this time to point out the cycle of Elijah's stories in the text (1 Kings 17:1—2 Kings 1:18). These stories give us a picture of the atmosphere of this period. One of the major sources of conflict was the importation of Baal worship in Israel. Ahab is a representative of the stance of the kings toward the worship of Baal. He and his predecessors and successors are presented by the authors of the books of Kings as responsible for leading Israel astray. Ahab was singled out as a chief offender.

Ahab was followed by Ahaziah (850–849 B.C.: 1 Kings 22:51—2 Kings 1:18), who reigned for a brief period. Ahaziah was followed by Jehoram, his brother (849–842 B.C.: 2 Kings 3:1-27). During Jehoram's reign the Moabites went to war against Israel. The unmerciful punishment Jehoram lashed upon the Moabites is illustrative of the violence of this period. Jehoram also permitted the Baal worship (2 Kings 8:18), and like Ahab, he was confronted by the prophet of God. This time the spokesman was Elisha. It was he who anointed Jehu king of Israel in the place of Joram (Jehoram), thereby beginning the purge of Ahab's house:

> Then Elisha the prophet called one of the sons of the prophets and said to him, "Gird up your loins, and take this flask of oil in your hand, and go to Ramoth-gilead. And when you arrive, look

there for Jehu the son of Jehoshaphat, son of Nimshi; and go in and bid him rise from among his fellows, and lead him to an inner chamber. Then take the flask of oil, and pour it on his head, and say, 'Thus says the Lord, I anoint you king over Israel.' Then open the door and flee; do not tarry" (2 Kings 9:1-3).

Purge of Jehu

Jehu was the righteous warrior who purged Israel of the idolatrous leadership of the house of Ahab. He slew all of the male heirs in addition to his assassination of Joram (Jehoram), the king of Israel (2 Kings 9:21-24), and Ahaziah, the king of Judah (2 Kings 9:27-28). Jehu continued his purge by ordering the death of Jezebel. Her attempt to tempt him seems rather modern, "When Jehu came to Jezreel, Jezebel heard of it; and she painted her eyes and adorned her head, and looked out of the window" (2 Kings 9:30). Nevertheless, he was not attracted by her makeup and ordered her thrown out the window:

He said, "Throw her down." So they threw her down; and some of her blood spattered on the wall and on the horses, and they trampled on her. Then he went in and ate and drank; and he said, "See now to this cursed woman, and bury her; for she is a king's daughter." But when they went to bury her, they found no more of her than the skull and the feet and the palms of her hands. When they came back and told him, he said, "This is the word of the Lord, which he spoke by his servant Elijah the Tishbite, 'In the territory of Jezreel the dogs shall eat the flesh of Jezebel; and the corpse of Jezebel shall be as dung upon the face of the field in the territory of Jezreel, so that no one can say, This is Jezebel'" (2 Kings 9:33-37).

This scene, too, seems modern and reflects the moral decline of this period of Israel's history as well as our own violent and oppressive humanity.

Jehu also slew the sons of Ahab (2 Kings 10:1-14), and later under the pretention that he was a devotee of Baal, he massacred the worshipers of Baal (2 Kings 10:18-28).

Having completed the purge, the chroniclers praised Jehu, but they also criticized:

But Jehu did not turn aside from the sins of Jeroboam the son of

Nebat, which he made Israel to sin, the golden calves that were in Bethel, and in Dan. And the Lord said to Jehu, "Because you have done well in carrying out what is right in my eyes, and have done to the house of Ahab according to all that was in my heart, your sons of the fourth generation shall sit on the throne of Israel." But Jehu was not careful to walk in the law of the Lord the God of Israel with all his heart; he did not turn from the sins of Jeroboam, which he made Israel to sin (2 Kings 10:29-31).

Unfortunately the purge of Jehu was too late and too little. Decline was already set and moral decadence was the order of the day. The demise of Israel and the subsequent fall of Judah had already begun.

When Jehu slew Ahaziah, Athaliah, his mother, seized the throne and became queen in Judah. In seeking to secure her position, she slew all of the heirs to the throne, except Jehoash (Joash), who was rescued by his aunt, the wife of Jehoida the priest (2 Kings 11:1-3). Athaliah ruled for six years until she was assassinated and Jehoash was made king (2 Kings 11:4-20). Although Jehoash rebuilt the temple and tried to restore order (2 Kings 11:21–12:21), Judah, like Israel, was in serious trouble, for internal chaos and external threats from foreign powers had already begun.

From Jehu's Purge to the Fall of the Northern Kingdom (842-722 B.C.)

Jehu's purge cleansed Israel of idolatry but also destroyed her leaders. Thus the internal stability of Israel was weakened beyond repair. Jehu's dynasty, which lasted for approximately one hundred years, never recovered from the debilitating effects of the terrible blood bath. The internal struggles were matched by the rise of foreign powers. The Assyrian armies had already begun to move. Both the internal weakness and the external threat from foreign powers formed the context for Israel during this century.

Jehu's dynasty was isolated and exposed to all kinds of difficulties. Hosea later suggested that Jehu's extermination of the house of Omri subjected Jehu to a guilt that God would avenge: "And the Lord said to him, 'Call his name Jezreel; for yet a little while, and I will punish the house of Jehu for the blood of Jezreel, and I will put an end to the kingdom of the house of Israel'" (Hosea 1:4).

Another aspect of the reign of Jehu was his payment of tribute to the Assyrian king Shalmaneser. The portrayal of this payment is seen in the famous so-called Black Obelisk, found in the royal city of Calah (Kalah) near modern Tell Nimrud. This is significant because it foretells of Israel's life during the next century.

Assyria was not to exert its full power at this time. Damascus served as a hedge. The ascending of Hazael to power in Damascus (the capital of Syria, to be distinguished from Assyria at this time in ancient history) provided this temporary barrier to Assyrian domination of Israel.

> And the Lord said to him, "Go, return on your way to the wilderness of Damascus; and when you arrive, you shall anoint Hazael to be king over Syria; and Jehu the son of Nimshi you shall anoint to be king over Israel; and Elisha the son of Shaphat of Abelmeholah you shall anoint to be prophet in your place. And him who escapes from the sword of Hazael shall Jehu slay; and him who escapes from the sword of Jehu shall Elisha slay" (1 Kings 19:15-17).

Hazael's usurpation of power under such dubious means was a threat to Israel. However, he was preoccupied with the threats which he received from Shalmaneser and the Assyrians. Later Shalmaneser withdrew from further interference, and this left Hazael to return his attention to Israel. Elisha the prophet sensed the danger when he told Hazael, ". . . I know the evil that you will do to the people of Israel; you will set on fire their fortresses, and you will slay their young men with the sword, and dash in pieces their little ones, and rip up their women with child" (2 Kings 8:12).

The threat of Damascus was ended in 800 B.C. when the Assyrian king, Adadnirare III, forced the king of Damascus into submission. This decline in the power of Damascus permitted Israel to experience a resurgence of independence. This brief period of respite from threat took place under Jehoash (801–786 B.C.), Jehu's grandson. The record of his rise to power is found in 2 Kings 14:1-14. Jehoash recovered the territories that had been taken by the Aramaeans west of the Jordan, and he also defeated Judah because of a misunderstanding between himself and the king of Judah, Amaziah, which grew out of Amaziah's decision not to use Israelite mercenaries in his battle with the Edomites.

The story of conflict between Jehoash (Joash) and Amaziah is found in 2 Chronicles 25 and is an example of the chaotic conditions that prevailed. Murder, bloodshed, and violence were the order of the day; even more was to follow.

Jehoash permitted Amaziah to return to Israel, but Amaziah was later assassinated and his son, Uzziah (Azariah), succeeded him (2 Kings 14:17-21).

Despite the dispute between the northern and southern kings, an uneasy peace prevailed in both Israel and Judah. The two kings who reigned during this time were Jeroboam II (786–746 B.C.: 2 Kings 14:23-29) in the north and Uzziah, also called Azariah (783–742 B.C.: 2 Kings 15:1-7), in the south. Jeroboam II was primarily a military figure, and he was able to expand his borders in the north through the defeat of Damascus and to eject the Moabites and Ammonites from Israelite territory. He at first overshadowed his younger contemporary Uzziah.

Uzziah began his reign at sixteen. He eventually came into his own as a king who had a long and successful career. He repaired the defense of Jerusalem (2 Chronicles 26:9, 11-15), reorganized the army, and began an aggressive campaign to expand the territories of Judah against Edom and the northwestern Arabian tribes.

These two men reigned over Israel and Judah in a time of prosperity that was second only to the golden age of David and Solomon. This was a time of relative peace at home, peace between each other, and peace from foreign interference. But this outward calm was not the whole story. Israel and Judah experienced moral sickness and internal decay. This experience is best articulated by the prophets who appeared on the scene in both kingdoms to declare to each her sin. The period of prosperity was soon to come to an end. Two simultaneous factors brought about the change in the state of affairs: the deaths of Jeroboam II and Uzziah (746 and 742 B.C.); and the rise to power of Assyria's great empire builder, Tiglath-pileser III (754–727 B.C.). His ascendancy marked the beginning of an Assyrian period in the nation's history. It is impossible to understand the experience of both kingdoms apart from these events.

Revival of the Assyrian Empire

Jeroboam II's death was followed by the inevitable. Political anarchy returned to the Northern Kingdom in a fashion similar to that of the early days of Jeroboam I. Five kings occupied the throne within a short period of ten years. Jeroboam's son, Zechariah, reigned only six months before he was murdered (c. 745 B.C.) by Shallum ben Jabesh. Shallum, in turn, was killed within one month by Menahem ben Gadi and Menahem then reigned. This political chaos opened the door for Tiglath-pileser III, ruler of Assyria, who had already begun the revival of the Assyrian empire. Menahem paid tribute to Tiglath-pileser as he made his march westward. These events are recorded in Second Kings, chapters 15 and 16.

The Assyrian king seized the throne with two goals: to reassert Assyrian power against the Aramean (Chaldean) people of Babylonia to the south and the Subartu kingdom to the north; and to subdue the other political powers in the west, namely Damascus, Syria, and Palestine. He eventually achieved these goals in the north and south; but before he completed these tasks, he made his westward conquest into Syria. At first he was thwarted, presumably by a coalition led by Uzziah; nevertheless, by 738 B.C. most of the states of northern Palestine, including Israel, were paying tribute to the Assyrian king. Assyria introduced a new strategy for dealing with conquered people. Tiglath-pileser's policy, in addition to receiving tributes and punishing the resisters, was to make his conquest permanent by deporting the leaders of the inhabitants and incorporating their lands within the Assyrian empire. This policy soon had its debilitating effects upon Israel. They soon would be exiled into Assyria. Israel's political chaos opened the door for conquest by Tiglath-pileser.

The Fall of the Northern Kingdom (Israel)

The political chaos described earlier continued when Menahem was unable to stabilize the throne. He was followed by his son, Pekahiah (738–737 B.C.), who in turn was assassinated by one of his officers, Pekah ben Remaliah. Pekah seized the throne and organized a coalition against Assyria which was soon demolished. His leadership of the anti-Assyrian coalition precipitated war with Judah, and this marked the beginning of the end for Israel.

The national character was destroyed and evil was rampant. The chaos that emerged is pictured by Hosea:

When I would restore the fortunes of my people,
    when I would heal Israel,
the corruption of Ephraim is revealed,
    and the wicked deeds of Samaria;
for they deal falsely,
    and the thief breaks in,
    and the bandits raid without.
But they do not consider
    that I remember all their evil works.
Now their deeds encompass them,
    they are before my face.
By their wickedness they make the king glad,
    and the princes by their treachery.
They are all adulterers;
    they are like a heated oven,
whose baker ceases to stir the fire,
    from the kneading of the dough until it is leavened.
On the day of our king the princes
    became sick with the heat of wine;
    he stretched out his hand with mockers.
For like an oven their hearts burn with intrigue;
    all night their anger smolders;
    in the morning it blazes like a flaming fire.
All of them are hot as an oven,
    and they devour their rulers.
And their kings have fallen;
    and none of them calls upon me.

—Hosea 7:1-7

Finally the political life was ended with the abortive attempt by Pekah to lead an Aramean-Israelite coalition against Assyria. The events are tragic to describe.

Pekah in cooperation with Rezin, the king of Damascus, wanted to resist the onslaught of Tiglath-pileser. They tried to persuade Jotham, king of Judah (742–735 B.C.), to join them. He refused and died while maintaining his independence. When Jotham's son, Ahaz, succeeded him, Pekah and his coalition invaded Judah and surrounded Jerusalem (2 Kings 16:5). Meanwhile, Edom, which had been subjected to Judah for the greater part of the eighth century, rebelled and regained its independence. Edom joined the coalition against Ahaz but felt constrained. In desperation Ahaz appealed to Tiglath-pileser for help. This critical period is described in Isaiah 7:1–8:22. Tiglath-pileser accepted Ahaz's call for help and completely destroyed the coalition.

Tiglath-pileser annihilated much in his path in his march down the seacoast through Israelite territory. He destroyed the Philistine cities, especially Gaza, which had been one of the leaders in the resistance. He attacked Israel a second time with full force destroying Galilee, the Transjordan, and numerous cities. Further, he deported many of the inhabitants. Meanwhile Pekah was murdered by Hoshea ben Elah (732–724 B.C.), who surrendered and paid tribute. This probably saved Israel from complete destruction.

Unfortunately, Hoshea's act only temporarily saved the city. He made overtures to Egypt and defected from paying tribute to Assyria when Tiglath-pileser was succeeded by his son Shalmaneser V. This was a terrible mistake and resulted in the death blow to Israel's independence. Shalmaneser attacked Hoshea and made him a prisoner. By 724 B.C. Israel became an occupied land with the exception of Samaria, which held on for two years. In the midst of the siege Shalmaneser died and was succeeded by Sargon II (722–705 B.C.), who finally subdued the city in 721 B.C. He completely destroyed Samaria and deported many of the citizens into a nameless existence in exile. Israel's political history was finished.

The Fall of the Southern Kingdom (Judah)

Judah now existed as a separate kingdom. This little kingdom continued under Assyrian domination until the rise of Nabopalassar, the first ruler of the neo-Babylonian empire. She then became subject to Babylon, in spite of her attempts to remain free.

The events of this period focus upon two kings, Hezekiah (2 Kings 18:1–20:21) and Josiah (2 Kings 22:1–23:30). The first king for our discussion is Hezekiah, who succeeded his father Ahaz and remained loyal to Assyria. He tried to initiate cultic reform and to have the northern inhabitants who remained worship at Jerusalem. His reforms and success in war are described thus:

He removed the high places, and broke the pillars, and cut down the Asherah. And he broke in pieces the bronze serpent that Moses had made, for until those days the people of Israel had burned incense to it; it was called Nehushtan. He trusted in the Lord the God of Israel; so that there was none like him among all the kings of Judah after him, nor among those who were before him. For he held fast to the Lord; he did not depart from following him, but kept the commandments which the Lord commanded Moses. And the Lord was with him; wherever he went forth, he prospered. He rebelled against the king of Assyria, and would not serve him. He smote the Philistines as far as Gaza and its territory, from watchtower to fortified city (2 Kings 18:4-8).

However, Hezekiah did not learn from the experience of his northern predecessors. When Sargon II was killed in battle, Sennacherib, his successor, was confronted by resistance in the east and west. Merodach-baladan (2 Kings 20:12-15; cf. Isaiah 39:1-4) established himself as king in Babylon and encouraged Judah to join him against Sennacherib. Egypt, which was gaining power in the twenty-fifth dynasty, promised to help. Other cities in Phoenicia and Philistia were also actively involved. This coalition failed just as Pekah's coalition failed and Judah was ravaged, but Jerusalem was spared (2 Kings 18:13-16; cf. chaps. 17–19).

Sennacherib sent a force against Jerusalem to destroy the city. Hezekiah resisted. While Hezekiah was resisting, Sennacherib heard of an approaching army from Egypt and had to turn his attention to fight this battle; thus, he sent a letter to Hezekiah to threaten him into submission. Meanwhile, the Assyrian army suffered a mysterious plague and this pestilence broke the back of the seige: "And that night the angel of the Lord went forth, and slew a hundred and eighty-five thousand in the camp of the Assyrians; and when men arose early in the morning, behold, these were all dead bodies. Then Sennacherib king of Assyria departed, and went home, and dwelt at Nineveh" (2 Kings 19:35-36). There was no question in the mind of the writer of the book of Kings that this plague was an act of God. Isaiah describes the celebration in the city of Jerusalem when the Assyrians withdrew:

> What do you mean that you have gone up,
>   all of you, to the housetops,
> you who are full of shoutings,

tumultuous city, exultant town?
Your slain are not slain with the sword
    or dead in battle.
All your rulers have fled together,
    without the bow they were captured.
All of you who were found were captured,
    though they had fled far away.
Therefore I said:
"Look away from me,
    let me weep bitter tears;
do not labor to comfort me
    for the destruction of the daughter of my people."
                                        —Isaiah 22:1-4

In spite of this temporary respite to Jerusalem, Judah was still in trouble. Isaiah also describes the havoc that had been wrought in the country:

Why will you still be smitten,
    that you continue to rebel?
The whole head is sick,
    and the whole heart faint.
From the sole of the foot even to the head,
    there is no soundness in it,
but bruises and sores
    and bleeding wounds;
they are not pressed out, or bound up,
    or softened with oil.

Your country lies desolate,
    your cities are burned with fire;
in your very presence
    aliens devour your land;
    it is desolate, as overthrown by aliens.
And the daughter of Zion is left
    like a booth in a vineyard,
like a lodge in a cucumber field,
    like a besieged city.

If the Lord of hosts

had not left us a few survivors,
we should have been like Sodom,
and become like Gomorrah.
                              —Isaiah 1:5-9

Other prophets whom we shall discuss in the next chapter also give us an understanding of this period. Let us now look at the final chapter in the political history of the divided kingdom.

Hezekiah was followed by his son Manasseh (687-642 B.C.: 2 Kings 21:1-18) who did not follow the religious reforms of his father. Instead Manasseh restored the high places and fertility cults and installed pagan altars in the temple at Jerusalem. He included the adoption of the Assyrian astral cult and human sacrifice. Manasseh was succeeded by his son Amon (642-640 B.C.: 2 Kings 21:20-22). Through palace intrigue he was assassinated, but Josiah, the eight-year-old son of Amon, was able to succeed his father (2 Kings 22:1-23:30). His discovery of the Book of Law made him the second significant king in the final days of Israel.

Hezekiah was known for his reform of the cultus, and Josiah was responsible for the renewal of the covenant and continuing the reform of the cultus (2 Kings 23:4-15). These reforms were most extensive and are described in great detail in the biblical text of 2 Kings 22, and 2 Chronicles 34. These reforms were influenced by the prophetic ideals that were enunciated by Amos, Hosea, Isaiah, and Micah. Before we discuss these prophetic ideals and the resulting reforms, let us conclude our discussion of the final days of Judah. Josiah's significance was not only related to the reforms but also to Judah's last experience with independence. This was tied up with the decline of the Assyrian empire.

Like the life cycle of all the preceding great powers, Assyria's star having risen began to fall. Her empire extended far beyond her ability of control, and therefore internal decay set in at the same time other world powers like Babylon and Egypt became restless. It is impossible to detail all of these events within this discussion; nevertheless, we know that eventually Assyria collapsed and the vassal states, including Judah, once again experienced freedom. This happened under the reign of Josiah, the reformer mentioned above.

Josiah's reforms and Assyria's demise did not prohibit the tragedy that was to follow. Judah's freedom was short-lived, and the reforms were more external than internal. The reforms did not restore the nation's spirit or revive its commitment to God.

The beginning of the tragic end of Judah began with the death of Josiah. He was killed in battle at Megiddo in 609 B.C. when he attempted to stop Neco II of Egypt (609–593 B.C.) who had joined with Asshur-uballit of Assyria in an effort to retake Haran from the Babylonians. His death is described in the tragic scene that follows:

> Before him there was no king like him, who turned to the Lord with all his heart and with all his soul and with all his might, according to all the law of Moses; nor did any like him arise after him.
>
> Still the Lord did not turn from the fierceness of his great wrath, by which his anger was kindled against Judah, because of all the provocations with which Manasseh had provoked him. And the Lord said, "I will remove Judah also out of my sight, as I have removed Israel, and I will cast off this city which I have chosen, Jerusalem, and the house of which I said, My name shall be there."
>
> Now the rest of the acts of Josiah, and all that he did, are they not written in the Book of the Chronicles of the Kings of Judah? In his days Pharaoh Neco king of Egypt went up to the king of Assyria to the river Euphrates. King Josiah went to meet him; and Pharaoh Neco slew him at Megiddo, when he saw him. And his servants carried him dead in a chariot from Megiddo, and brought him to Jerusalem, and buried him in his own tomb. And the people of the land took Jehoahaz the son of Josiah, and anointed him, and made him king in his father's stead (2 Kings 23:25-30).

His son Jehoahaz succeeded him to the kingship (2 Kings 23:31-34) and became involved in the ongoing struggle between Neco II and the Babylonians. Although Neco II, the Egyptians' prince, lost in his attempt to retake Haran, he proceeded to solidify his position west of the Euphrates. This included Judah. He did this by deposing Jehoahaz, who had reigned only three months, and placing his brother Eliakim, whose name was changed to Jehoiakim, on the throne as a vassal of the Pharaoh of Egypt (2 Kings 23:36–24:6).

Jehoiakim was ordered to pay heavy tribute to Egypt through a head tax on all free citizens. He was apparently a poor king and provoked the contempt of Jeremiah (Jeremiah 22:18-19). He was unable to maintain the reforms instituted under Josiah. Chaos

seemed imminent. In addition to subjugation by Egypt and
Jehoiakim's internal struggles, another international power struggle
presented Judah with a new threat. This time the vigorous new leader
was Nebuchadnezzar of Babylonia.

Nebuchadnezzar attacked and defeated the Egyptian force at
Carchemish in 605 B.C. and established Babylon as a new force to be
contended with for world power. He defeated them a second time
near Hamath. Upon hearing of the death of his father, Nabupolassar,
Nebuchadnezzar returned home to assume the kingship. This only
delayed briefly the march of the Babylonian forces. When Judah saw
the Babylonian destruction of the Philistine plain and the deportation of the citizens of Ashkelon (Jeremiah 47:5-7), she panicked as she
awaited her fate:

> Look among the nations, and see;
>> wonder and be astounded.
> For I am doing a work in your days
>> that you would not believe if told.
> For lo, I am rousing the Chaldeans,
>> that bitter and hasty nation,
> who march through the breadth of the earth,
>> to seize habitations not their own.
> Dread and terrible are they;
>> their justice and dignity proceed from themselves.
> Their horses are swifter than leopards,
>> more fierce than the evening wolves;
>> their horsemen press proudly on.
> Yea, their horsemen come from afar;
>> they fly like an eagle swift to devour.
> They all come for violence;
>> terror of them goes before them.
>> They gather captives like sand.
> At kings they scoff,
>> and of rulers they make sport.
> They laugh at every fortress,
>> for they heap up earth and take it.
> Then they sweep by like the wind and go on,
>> guilty men, whose own might is their god!
> —Habakkuk 1:5-11; cf. Jeremiah 46:1; 4:5-8; 5:15-17; 6:22-26

This turn of events resulted in Jehoiakim's reluctant submission to Nebuchadnezzar, and once again Judah was subject to a Mesopotamian power.

Jehoiakim's unwilling vassalage proved to be Judah's downfall. When Nebuchadnezzar's march against Egypt did not result in a decisive victory, Jehoiakim thought there was hope for Judah in an alliance with Egypt. He rebelled against Nebuchadnezzar who did not respond immediately to this threat. But in 598 B.C., Nebuchadnezzar sent the Babylonian army on its bloody march. During the same month, Jehoiakim died and Jehoiachin, his eighteen-year-old son, succeeded him. Within three months Jerusalem surrendered, and Jehoiachin the king of Judah, his mother, the high officials, and other leading citizens and inhabitants were taken into Babylon. The scene is a tragic one chronicled in 2 Kings 24. Judah was left with a shell of her former self. Mattaniah (Zedekiah), Jehoiachin's uncle, was made king over what remained.

The end of Judah's nationhood was precipitated by Zedekiah's continual agitation and sedition. Judah had been severely weakened by Jehoiachin's unwise policies, and Zedekiah was unable to handle such a difficult situation. His unstable position worsened when he misread the meaning of a rebellion by Jews and prophets in Babylon in 594 B.C. (Jeremiah 29). He planned a revolt with the ambassadors of Edom, Moab, Ammon, and Tyre. However, this revolt never materialized; nevertheless, within five years the final step was taken. Inflamed by false hopes of support from Egypt and false hopes for a swift return of the exiles, Judah rebelled in open defiance. Nebuchadnezzar responded with full force. He put a blockade around Jerusalem and began to attack the outlying posts one by one. While his army was moving closer and closer, Judah was temporarily relieved by news that an Egyptian contingent was advancing. Judah hoped for success of this Egyptian movement, but Jeremiah realistically predicted the fall of the city. The Egyptians were defeated, and Jerusalem lay isolated and helpless. Although Zedekiah wished to surrender, the fanatic zeal of the nationalists in Jerusalem made them fight to the end. Zedekiah tried to escape with a few of his officers, but he was apprehended, and, having witnessed the death of his sons, he was blinded and sent to prison in Babylon where he died.

The story ends with the reign of Gedaliah as governor (2 Kings 25:22-26). Jerusalem was completely destroyed; the land was spoiled; the economy was devastated; and the outstanding citizens were killed. The Babylonians appointed Gedaliah to serve as governor of the ruined, devastated remains. He moved the seat to Mizpah probably because Jerusalem was uninhabitable. Soon he was assassinated as a collaborator. His death was a symbol of Judah and the kingdom that was the glory of David. It was dead, never to rise again.

In this chapter we have discussed at some length the period of the divided kingdom. This was the transition from order to chaos. Although there were periodic attempts to recover the glory of the Davidic period, that day never arrived. This period was characterized by the declining of the monarchy, but through God's will it was the period of the beginning of classical prophecy, that aspect of Israel's life that really makes the Old Testament a part of the church's book of faith.

QUESTIONS FOR FURTHER CONSIDERATION

• What were the advantages of having an order, or process, for the succession of rulers, as in the kingdom of Judah? What were the disadvantages? Are such rules and procedures necessary today?

• The biblical writers held the kings responsible for the moral and religious life of the nation. To what degree are national leaders today responsible for the moral tone of the nation?

• Why did the religious reforms under Josiah fail to halt the decline of the nation? How does this experience relate to the appeal today to save the nation by religious revival?

• How can we discern God's activity in the rise and fall of nations in the modern world?

The Divided Kingdom:
The Understanding and
Crossing Point
Chapter 8

In the last chapter we looked at the experience of the Hebrew people during the time of the divided kingdom and the final destruction of Israel and Judah. This discussion focused primarily upon the political history of the kings as summarized in the books of First and Second Kings. The experience which these books articulate was one of internal disintegration, crisis, external threats, and apostasy. The persons who understood this period best were the class of individuals referred to as the prophets. They were sensitive to the meaning of what was going on and tried to communicate God's message in this time of internal turmoil and external threat. Their familiar word of authority was: "Thus saith the Lord."

THE UNDERSTANDING

The prophets' understanding of this period can be summarized by James Russell Lowell's poignant statement, "Every man feels instinctively that all the beautiful sentiments in the world weigh less than a single lovely action." The true meaning of religion is belief and action, or as Micah put it:

> "He has showed you, O man, what is good;
>   and what does the Lord require of you
> but to do justice, and to love kindness,
>   and to walk humbly with your God?"
> —Micah 6:8

The principal prophets for our discussion are Amos, Hosea, Jeremiah, and Isaiah. These are the principal prophets who are known as the literary or classical prophets. Scholars are generally agreed that the Hebrew word *nabî* comes from an Akkadian root which means "one sent" or one made to speak. The meaning that the Hebrew derives from this root is "spokesman."

Hebrew tradition traces the beginnings of prophecy to Moses (Numbers 11:24-30). There are several other persons to whom this term is applied. In addition to Moses and Aaron (Exodus 7:1 and Numbers 12:2-8), Miriam (Exodus 15:20) and Deborah (Judges 4:4) are called prophets by the writers of three of the biblical narratives.

Historically the prophets can be traced to the tenth century B.C. during the late period of the judges and the early monarchy. These persons were ecstatics and were known primarily for their religious fervor. They were often identified as a "group" and known as "sons of the prophets" (1 Samuel 10:6-8; 10-13; 1 Kings 20:35; 2 Kings 2:3). Samuel was identified with such a group or guild of prophets (1 Samuel 19:20). Elijah and Elisha are also represented with the ecstatic dimension of Israelite prophecy.

Although ecstaticism remained a part of Israelite prophecy, the prophets who represented the distinctive dimension of Hebrew prophecy focused upon the message from God. It was not their ecstatic behavior that authenticated their role as prophets, but their special sense of God's presence, evidenced in their call and message.

A seminary student shared in a chapel service a story which places in perspective the role of the classical prophets:

> As the clown was about to go into the ring to perform, the manager noticed that the tent had caught fire. He told the clown: "Say to the people that the tent is on fire, and that they shall all perish unless they leave now in an orderly manner." The clown jumped into the ring and shouted: "The tent is on fire! The tent is on fire!" The people, seeing it was the clown shouting, thought it was all a great joke and started laughing. The louder he shouted, the more they laughed. And they all perished.

Unfortunately, Israel, like the people in the story, refused to heed the words of the prophets in spite of the fact that they spoke from a sense of urgency from God. The classical prophet felt a special call from God to declare his truth. The significance of the prophets was first and foremost their sense of being spokesmen for God with a message of life or death. They spoke from the context of their own situation and own traditions with a message that became the judgment and conscience of the people, but they came with a message that the people refused to heed.

The prophets under consideration did not create a new religion. What they did was to interpret the meaning of God, of the covenant, of faith for their day. Isaiah's parable of the vineyard is illustrative of the pathos of the prophets' message.

Let me sing for my beloved
  a love song concerning his vineyard:
My beloved had a vineyard
  on a very fertile hill.
He digged it and cleared it of stones,
  and planted it with choice vines;
he built a watchtower in the midst of it,
  and hewed out a wine vat in it;
and he looked for it to yield grapes,
  but it yielded wild grapes.

And now, O inhabitants of Jerusalem
  and men of Judah,
judge, I pray you, between me and my vineyard.
What more was there to do for my vineyard,
  that I have not done in it?
When I looked for it to yield grapes,
  why did it yield wild grapes?

And now I will tell you
  what I will do to my vineyard.
I will remove its hedge,
  and it shall be devoured;
I will break down its wall,
  and it shall be trampled down.
I will make it a waste;
  it shall not be pruned or hoed,
  and briers and thorns shall grow up;
I will also command the clouds
  that they rain no rain upon it.

For the vineyard of the Lord of hosts
  is the house of Israel,
and the men of Judah
  are his pleasant planting;

> and he looked for justice,
> but behold, bloodshed;
> for righteousness,
> but behold, a cry!
> —Isaiah 5:1-7

These introductory comments also enable us to gain a clearer picture of the prophets' vehement denunciation of social corruption. Such crimes as dispossessing and impoverishing the masses and living wantonly and luxuriously were added to idolatry as the cause of social dissolution.

This state of societal decay was very much in evidence during the period of the monarchy and the centuries following its rise. New rights of kings to confiscate property supplemented the ancient methods of inheriting property. Also there arose a new class of officials who were connected with the courts. These factors introduced a sharp cleavage in the society that was once based on close ties of families and tribes. Into this setting the prophets thundered God's word to his people. The prophets spoke God's word of judgment and hope. Although their historical settings were different, they spoke with a consistent oneness on God's demand for justice and righteousness.

B. Davie Napier, has given a meaningful outline of the classical prophetism in the period studied. He suggests that the classical prophets can be understood in terms of the question of judgment. Their underlying theme is God's judgment against Israel. This jugment is not based upon their lack of religious practices but upon their failure to "do justly, to love mercy, and to walk humbly with God." Under the heading of judgment, he outlines the classical prophets as follows:

A. Anticipated Judgment: The Eighth Century
  1. Prophetism and the Eighth-Century Indictment: Amos 1–9
  2. Contingency and Compassion: Amos; Hosea 1–14
  3. The Theological Ethic and History: Isaiah 1–23; 28–33; Micah 1–7
B. Suspended Judgment: The Seventh Century
  1. Packaged Prophetism: Deuteronomy
  2. Faith and the Uncertain Present: Nahum 1–3; Zephaniah 1–3; Habakkuk 1–3

3. Protesting Prophetism: Jeremiah 1–52
C. Applied Judgment: The Sixth Century
   1. Hope and Bitterness: Jeremiah, Obadiah, Lamentations
   2. Insight and Resurrection: Ezekiel[1]

This outline by Napier helps us to contextualize the different periods in which the prophets "thundered forth God's mighty word." It also helps us to focus on the theme of their message. Napier's outline makes it clear that God was disappointed with Israel: she had broken the covenant; she had transgressed God's laws; she had missed the mark. This is the ethos into which the prophets entered. In the midst of broken dreams and deferred expectations the prophets spoke their message from God; Amos, the shepherd from Tekoa, was among the first to speak in the eighth century.

Amos

Amos prophesied during the reign of Jeroboam II of Israel (774–739 B.C.) and Uzziah of Judah (774–739 B.C.). Although he was from the Southern Kingdom, he appeared before the altar at Bethel in the north. The major thrust of Amos's message was that morality, not ritual, was the divine requirement. Amos began with a list of indictments against the surrounding countries—Damascus, Gaza, Tyre, Edom, Ammon, and Moab. Then he proceeded with a list of indictments against Judah:

> Thus says the Lord:
> "For three transgressions of Judah,
>   and for four, I will not revoke the punishment;
> because they have rejected the law of the Lord,
>   and have not kept his statutes,
> but their lies have led them astray,
>   after which their fathers walked.
> So I will send a fire upon Judah,
>   and it shall devour the strongholds of Jerusalem."
> —Amos 2:4-5

By beginning with the countries outside of Israel, Amos called attention to the fact that God is not just Lord of Israel; he is Lord of all the earth. Amos prefaced his oracular indictments with the prophetic formula, "Thus said the Lord." God is speaking to all the nations.

But Amos's focus was upon Israel, and he analyzed her existence as alienated and therefore unsatisfactory to God. He cried out against Israel's sin. He declared that she was under the terrible wrath of God.

> Thus says the Lord:
>   "For three transgressions of Israel,
>   and for four, I will not revoke the punishment;
>   because they sell the righteous for silver,
>   and the needy for a pair of shoes—."
>
> —Amos 2:6

Amos pronounced the death sentence. He illustrated these pronouncements of judgment with the three visions of the locust, fire, and plumb line (chapter 7) and predicted the final doom of Israel in the vision of summer fruit (chapters 8 and 9).

Amos's passionate and unrelieved condemnation were based upon his understanding of Israel's past, his understanding of the meaning of religion. First, he saw Israel's social and religious structure as being corrupt. Israel's past history was evidence of her unfaithfulness to God. The social structure permitted the oppressors to:

1. "store up violence and robbery in their strongholds" (3:10)
2. "oppress the poor . . . crush the needy" (4:1b)
3. "turn justice to wormwood, and cast down righteousness to the earth!" (5:7)
4. "hate him who reproves in the gate . . . abhor him who speaks the truth" (5:10)
5. "trample upon the poor and take from him exactions of wheat" (5:11a)
6. "afflict the righteous, who take a bribe, and turn aside the needy in the gate" (5:12b).

The life-style of the oppressors led them to assume that they were at ease at the expense of the oppressed. But Amos warned them:

> "Woe to those who are at ease in Zion,
>   and to those who feel secure on
>   the mountain of Samaria,
>   the notable men of the first of the nations,
>   to whom the house of Israel come!"
>
> —Amos 6:1

Not only was the social structure evil, but also the religious practices and commitment of the people were equally corrupt. There was no correlation between their moral life and religious practices (Amos 4:4-5; 5:21-23). These past and present practices were denounced by Amos. They were antithetical to his understanding of religion.

For Amos, religion could be summed up in the following words, "But let justice roll down like waters, and righteousness like an ever-flowing stream" (5:24). This view of religion is integral to the message of this prophet. Gross sins, such as murder, sexual immorality, oppression of strangers, inhuman cruelty, and the like, are the usual types of sins. But Amos goes deeper. He identifies perversion of justice, bribe taking, exploitation of the poor, and other forms of injustice as subject to God's judgment. God demands his followers be like him. Therefore, justice, righteousness, kindness, and compassion are the virtues of the people of God.

This understanding of religion led Amos to proclaim doom. He reinterpreted the meaning of the "Day of the Lord." In Amos's day this phrase meant Israel's deliverance from the oppression of her enemies and her triumph over them. Amos rejected this conception of the Day of the Lord and thundered forth that it would be a time of doom.

> Woe to you who desire the day of the Lord!
>   Why would you have the day of the Lord?
> It is darkness, and not light;
>   as if a man fled from a lion,
>   and a bear met him;
> or went into the house and leaned
>   with his hand against the wall,
>   and a serpent bit him.
> Is not the day of the Lord darkness, and not light,
>   and gloom with no brightness in it?
> —Amos 5:18-20

Therefore, Amos called Israel to repent, to return to God. Repentance was their only hope.

As one reads the prophecy of Amos, one hears the voice of the man of God, warning the people of their sin. Although these prophecies are harsh, they were spoken not out of hostility but out of Amos's irresistible call. He states that he was not a prophet nor a prophet's son, but he was just a shepherd who was constrained by the call of God. In response to a rebuke by Amaziah, the priest at Bethel, he replied:

> . . . "I am no prophet, nor a prophet's son; but I am a herdsman, and a dresser of sycamore trees, and the Lord took me from following the flock, and the Lord said to me, 'Go, prophesy to my people Israel.'" (Amos 7:14-15)

Amos's predicament is similar to the responsible citizen in Ibsen's *An Enemy of the People.* Thomas Stockmann discovered that the town baths, which were a basic source of revenue for the city, were leaking a gas that was a threat to the health of the city. This knowledge compelled the doctor to warn the town officers and the people concerning this imminent danger to their health. Although he was eventually rejected by the leaders of the town, he felt it was his responsibility to "tell the truth." This was the task of Amos. God had revealed to him that Israel was in serious trouble. His prophecies were a warning for her to return to God.

This plea for a return to God is a part of Amos's message of consolation. He sees the remnant (9:8-10) as those persons who because of their righteousness will survive. Although the later prophets made the remnant apply to all, including Gentiles, the text in Amos does not necessarily suggest this concept. Amos cried for Israel to return to God. He, like Hosea, spoke God's word to Israel. For both of them judgment was redemptive; it was through chastisement that Israel would be healed.

Hosea

The period which Hosea sought to understand was beset with turmoil and constant usurpation by would-be leaders whom the people could not respect. Politically Israel shifted between Egypt and Assyria in an attempt to remain alive.

Hosea's prophetic career followed Amos by several years, between the end of the reign of Jeroboam II (786–746 B.C.) and the fall of Damascus to Assyria in 737 B.C. Hosea's career parallels what Georg Fohrer suggests as the four distinct stages in the prophetical experience and ministry:

1. a moment of deep personal contact with God
2. the prophet's interpretation of his experience
3. the prophet's translation of the experience into rational and comprehensible words
4. the reduction of the words of a poetical structured form.

Hosea's experience follows this pattern. Hosea recorded his call from God: "When the Lord first spoke through Hosea, the Lord said to Hosea, 'Go, take to yourself a wife of harlotry and have children of harlotry, for the land commits great harlotry by forsaking the Lord'" (Hosea 1:2). We are not given the details of Hosea's call, but this text is sufficient to indicate that there was this initial contact or personal experience with God. He later interpreted this experience in his relationship with his wife.

Hosea in similar fashion to Isaiah, Jeremiah, Ezekiel, and Zechariah performed symbolic actions to emphasize his message. Hosea's marriages were symbolic acts to supplement his words. They dramatized God's message.

So he went and took Gomer the daughter of Diblaim, and she conceived and bore him a son.

And the Lord said to him, "Call his name Jezreel; for yet a little while, and I will punish the house of Jehu for the blood of Jezreel, and I will put an end to the kingdom of the house of Israel. And on that day, I will break the bow of Israel, in the valley of Jezreel."

She conceived again and bore a daughter. And the Lord said to him, "Call her name Not pitied, for I will no more have pity on the house of Israel, to forgive them at all. But I will have pity on the house of Judah, and I will deliver them by the Lord their God; I will not deliver them by bow, nor by sword, nor by war, nor by horses, nor by horsemen."

When she had weaned Not pitied, she conceived and bore a son. And the Lord said, "Call his name Not my people, for you are not my people and I am not your God."

Yet the number of the people of Israel shall be like the sand of the sea, which can be neither measured nor numbered; and in the place where it was said to them, "You are not my people," it shall be said to them, "Sons of the living God" (Hosea 1:3-10).

And the Lord said to me, "Go again, love a woman who is

beloved of a paramour and is an adulteress; even as the Lord loves the people of Israel, though they turn to other gods and love cakes of raisins." So I bought her for fifteen shekels of silver and a homer and a lethech of barley. And I said to her, "You must dwell as mine for many days; you shall not play the harlot, or belong to another man; so will I also be to you." For the children of Israel shall dwell many days without king or prince, without sacrifice or pillar, without ephod or teraphim. Afterward the children of Israel shall return and seek the Lord their God, and David their king; and they shall come in fear to the Lord and to his goodness in the latter days (Hosea 3:1-5).

In the first passage, Hosea was instructed to marry a "wife of harlotry," who begot children with the symbolic names "Jezreel," "Not pitied," and "Not my people." In the second text, Hosea was instructed to marry "an adulteress" who would sit in solitary confinement.

Many scholars have tried to understand these two passages. The range of opinion is from the position that this passage was an allegory to the belief that this was not the experience of the writer of Hosea 4–14. The present author feels that the traditional position that these two passages are two versions of the same story is a plausible interpretation. Hosea saw his marriage to Gomer as symbolic of Israel's relationship with God.

This is one of the main points of focus in Hosea's message. Gomer was unfaithful; Israel was unfaithful to God.

"And in that day, says the Lord, you will call me, 'My husband,' and no longer will you call me, 'My Baal.' For I will remove the names of the Baals from her mouth, and they shall be mentioned by name no more. And I will make for you a covenant on that day with the beasts of the field, the birds of the air, and the creeping things of the ground; and I will abolish the bow, the sword, and war from the land; and I will make you lie down in safety. And I will betroth you to me for ever; I will betroth you to me in righteousness and in justice, in steadfast love, and in mercy. I will betroth you to me in faithfulness; and you shall know the Lord" (Hosea 2:16-20).

The background for this comparison is the tension between God's faithfulness to Israel and Israel's unfaithfulness to God. Her infidelity was seen in her attempt to combine worship of Baal with the worship of God (Hosea 9:10). Amos attacked the cult because it was not undergirded by moral principles; Hosea attacked the cult because it was not focused upon God. Hosea goes further and gives the cause for Israel's unfaithfulness.

Israel's apostasy is due to the fact that loyalty, steadfastness, and knowledge of God are absent from the land. These are the three keys that help to appropriate Hosea's understanding of this period. Israel had lost a sense of the "presence of God," and thus her fall was imminent. These three terms are critical for our understanding of Hosea.

Hosea said there was no faithfulness in the land. Hosea reminded Israel of God's loyalty, the fact that he brought them out of the land of Egypt. Yet Israel worshiped Baal.

> Their deeds do not permit them to return to their God.
> For the spirit of harlotry is within them,
>   and they know not the Lord.
>
> —Hosea 5:4

Israel was unfaithful to the relationship that God had expected of her. Her faithlessness was seen in her lack of unlimited trust in God.

Israel was unfaithful to God in that she did not respond as God had expected. Hosea used the term *hesed* to describe the relationship which God expected. *Hesed* has been defined as loyalty, faithfulness, kindness, steadfast love. This word indicates the intimate relationship which God expected Israel to share with him. Hosea illustrated this unfaithfulness in his broken marriage with Gomer. It is Hosea's way of describing the core of the religious life. *Hesed* is the love of God which God desires from Israel. Thus God exclaims:

> For I desire steadfast love [*hesed*] and not
>   sacrifice,
> the knowledge of God, rather than burnt offerings.
>
> —Hosea 6:6

Hesed—loving-kindness—mercy—the fundamental quality which undergirds all right action was missing from Israel.

In addition to *hesed*, Hosea emphasized lack of knowledge of God as one aspect of Israel's sin.

> My people are destroyed for lack of knowledge;
>   because you have rejected knowledge,
> I reject you from being a priest to me.
> And since you have forgotten the law of your God,
>   I also will forget your children.
>
> —Hosea 4:6

George Adam Smith, noted biblical scholar, has given a lucid interpretation of Hosea's use of knowledge: "It is not to know so as to see the fact of, but to know so as to feel the force of: knowledge not as an acquisition but as an impression."[2]

On the one hand, Israel was given to sexual desanctification and drunkenness. These two evils are seen by the prophets as blinding Israel to the knowledge of God (Hosea 7:3-7). Harlotry and intoxication corrupt the mind and destroy the body. They forge a barrier between God and his people.

On the other hand, Hosea echoes Samuel's wrath against the monarchy:

> All of them are hot as an oven,
>   and they devour their rulers.
> All their kings have fallen;
>   and none of them calls upon me.
>
> —Hosea 7:7

However, the reason for his repudiation of the monarchy is threefold: (1) the anarchy of the times, (2) the rise of would-be saviors, (3) the negative attitude of the monarchs toward God and in his place dependence upon its defenses and militarism. Yehezkel Kaufmann rightly points out that Hosea was "The first biblical author, indeed the first man in history, to condemn militarism as a religious-moral sin. . . ."[3] Dependence upon military might was evidence that Israel did not have the knowledge of God. In spite of foreign alliances, Hosea warned:

> You have plowed iniquity,
>   you have reaped injustice,
>   you have eaten the fruit of lies.
> Because you have trusted in your chariots
>   and in the multitude of your warriors.
>
> —Hosea 10:13

Hosea sees punishment, but he also offers a word of hope.

The message of Hosea is one of punishment *and hope*. Destruction will come, but if Israel repents and returns to God, they will receive mercy. This is what Hosea meant by knowledge of God. Israel was not in intimate conversation with God; she was alienated. Her types of behavior manifested this lack of intimacy with God.

> Return, O Israel, to the Lord your God,
>   for you have stumbled because of your iniquity.
> Take with you words
>   and return to the Lord;
> say to him,
>   "Take away all iniquity;
> accept that which is good
>   and we will render
>   the fruit of our lips."
>
> —Hosea 14:1-2

This emphasis is what makes Hosea's message different from Amos's. Both declare punishment, but Hosea emphasizes God's mercy. Just as Hosea was willing to forgive Gomer and accept her back upon her return to him, so is God willing to accept Israel if she returns.

In the play *Green Pastures,* following God's judgment upon his people, a delegation goes to heaven and makes an appointment to see him. When they make known their request, they state, "Give us Hosea's God." While the message is being given, one hears the mobs and the hammers of the crucifixion. In brilliant juxtaposition, the author of *Green Pastures* makes us aware that God's sending of Jesus Christ is the embodiment of Hosea's message (Hosea 2:16-23). Hosea is the prophet of love. He was joined by Isaiah in his insistence that in the midst of God's judgment he offers love and pardon.

Isaiah

Isaiah is the third of the classical prophets who helps us to understand this period of Hebrew history. Let us briefly review the historical context in which his ministry took place, following the reigns of Jeroboam II (Northern Kingdom) and Uzziah (Southern Kingdom), internal threats and external crises. Approximately ten years after their deaths, Pekah, a successor of Jeroboam II, joined with Rezin the king of Aram in trying to coerce Ahaz, the successor of Jotham, to join with them in an abortive attempt to resist Tiglath-pileser of Assyria (745–727 B.C.). Ahaz refused and became a vassal of Assyria. In the meantime, Tiglath-pileser destroyed Damascus, the Aramaean capital, and later Israel was exiled by Sargon II, the successor of Tiglath-pileser. Ahaz of Judah was killed in battle, and Hezekiah, his son, succeeded him.

Hezekiah, the son of Ahaz, participated in similar abortive moves which brought calamity upon Judah. In 713–711 B.C. Judah and its neighbors revolted against Assyria. They were joined by Merodach-haladan of Babylonia with additional help provided by Egypt. In 711 and 710 B.C. this revolt was crushed. Another revolt by Judah was attempted when Sennacherib (705–681 B.C.) came to the throne in 705 B.C. But in 701 B.C. Sennacherib crushed the rebellion. Although Hezekiah paid tribute to Sennacherib, he refused to permit the Assyrians to occupy the city. Isaiah's ministry took place during these hectic and tumultuous days.

His call came after the great ruler Uzziah (742 B.C.) had died:

In the year that King Uzziah died I saw the Lord sitting upon a throne, high and lifted up; and his train filled the temple. Above him stood the seraphim; each had six wings: with two he covered his face, and with two he covered his feet, and with two he flew. And one called to another and said:

"Holy, holy, holy is the Lord of hosts;
the whole earth is full of his glory."

And the foundations of the thresholds shook at the voice of him who called, and the house was filled with smoke. And I said, "Woe is me! For I am lost; for I am a man of unclean lips, and I dwell in the midst of a people of unclean lips; for my eyes have seen the King, the Lord of hosts!"

Then flew one of the seraphim to me, having in his hand a burning coal which he had taken with tongs from the altar. And he touched my mouth, and said: "Behold, this has touched your lips; your guilt is taken away, and your sin forgiven." And I heard the voice of the Lord saying, "Whom shall I send, and who will go for us?" Then I said, "Here am I! Send me" (Isaiah 6:1-8).

The significant factor about Isaiah's call is that he intercepted a general call. Note that verse 8 indicates a general call, but Isaiah's experience forced him to say, "Here am I!" This acceptance of the prophetic ministry called him into a long career that lasted more than fifty years. John Bright evaluates the significance of Isaiah when he states: ". . . he towered over the contemporary scene and, though perhaps few in his day realized it, more than any other individual, guided the nation through her hour of tragedy and crisis."[4]

From Isaiah's call to the time before the Syro-Ephraimite war (746 or 740–736 B.C.) his focus was upon the social and ethical situation in Judah (chapters 1–5). His passionate oracles remind one of the thundering denunciations of Amos. He confronted the wealthy and powerful nobles and unscrupulous judges who exploited the poor and helpless (cf. Isaiah 1:21-23; 3:13-15; 10:1-4). These passages get at the heart of Isaiah's ethical message. Israel is under judgment—her kings, the government, and the people. All are subject to the divine wrath. Their only choice is to repent:

> "If you are willing and obedient,
>   you shall eat the good of the land;
> But if you refuse and rebel,
>   you shall be devoured by the sword;
>   for the mouth of the Lord has spoken."
>   —Isaiah 1:19-20

Isaiah, like Hosea, is a prophet of hope, and following his call to repentance he presents what Kaufmann calls "one of the noblest expressions of Israelite religion."[5]

The word which Isaiah the son of Amoz saw concerning Judah and Jerusalem.
> It shall come to pass in the latter days
>   that the mountain of the house of the Lord
> shall be established as the highest of the mountains,
>   and shall be raised above the hills;
> and all the nations shall flow to it.
>   —Isaiah 2:1-2

This vision depicts the end of idolatry and marks the beginning of a universal dimension to Israelite prophecy. Judgment will purify Israel's pride and arrogance, and God will be worshiped by all people.

Haughtiness will be done away with (cf. Isaiah 2:11-12, 17-18).

In these passages we have the picture of universal religion and universal morality. Worship of God will be combined with justice to the neighbor. This vision by Isaiah deals with the major evils which he attacked in the first period of his ministry: idolatrous pride and obsession with power which saw their manifestation in the appalling corruption of the middle class and the tremendous gap between the pompous wealthy and the miserable poor.

Isaiah shifts the focus of his message in the next period of his ministry. His messages are addressed primarily to the historical situation in which the Assyrians were attacking Syria and Palestine and when these states were doing all they could to survive. Specifically these prophecies were uttered when Ahaz refused to join the alliance against Tiglath-pileser (734 B.C.). The bulk of these prophecies are found in chapters 7–12. Isaiah opposed the alliance and Ahaz's decision to become a vassal of Assyria. His basis for his stand was his conviction that such involvement dims God's lordship of history. He pleaded with Israel to trust in God because human alliances would fail.

> "Thus says the Lord God:
>   It shall not stand,
>   and it shall not come to pass.
>   For the head of Syria is Damascus,
>   and the head of Damascus is Rezin.
>   (Within sixty-five years Ephraim will be broken to pieces
>   so that it will no longer be a people.)
>   And the head of Ephraim is Samaria.
>   and the head of Samaria is the son of Remaliah.
>   If you will not believe,
>   surely you shall not be established."
>
> —Isaiah 7:7-9

Nevertheless, God would redeem his people. Isaiah bursts forth into one of the classic passages which has been interpreted in light of God's role of Redeemer of his people. This passage undergirds Isaiah's contention that Judah should not depend upon foreign alliances but should trust in God.

For to us a child is born,
  to us a son is given;
and the government will be upon his shoulder,
  and his name will be called
"Wonderful Counselor, Mighty God,
  Everlasting Father, Prince of Peace."
Of the increase of his government and of peace
  there will be no end,
upon the throne of David, and over his kingdom,
  to establish it, and to uphold it
with justice and with righteousness
  from this time forth and for evermore.
The zeal of the Lord of hosts will do this.
                                    —Isaiah 9:6-7

The main point of this passage is that the meaning of true religion is faith in God. God will provide a means for delivering his people. Over and over again Judah is warned, "If you will not believe, surely you shall not be established" (Isaiah 7:9; cf. 7:10-15; 8:5). Only a remnant would survive the calamity that awaited those who would not put their complete trust in God.

Later Isaiah returned to active prophecy during the reign of Hezekiah, the son of Ahaz (Isaiah 10:5-12:6). He gave three oracles concerning Assyria. First (Isaiah 10:5-15), he saw Assyria as God's "rod of anger . . . against a godless nation." However, Isaiah changed his mind. He notes that this new king has in his mind ". . . to destroy and to cut off nations not a few" (Isaiah 10:7). The arrogance of this king portends his own destruction, for the prophet assures us that " . . . he will punish the arrogant boasting of the king of Assyria and his haughty pride" (Isaiah 10:12).

In the second oracle (Isaiah 10:15-34), Assyria is destroyed as the prophet had predicted. Assyria's sin is arrogant boasting and haughty pride. God will destroy this king and all who oppose him (Isaiah 10:24-27)! The third oracle treats the rise of a new king in the Davidic dynasty (Isaiah 11:1-12:6). After the storm, the calm! From the trauma of Assyria, God again affirms his lordship of history and his presence with his people. The new ruler will be of God's own choosing. His attributes will not be military might but "the Spirit of the Lord." He will be a just and righteous ruler who will bring in a new order (Isaiah 11:3-9). This vision reminds one of chapter 2. The natural order will be changed; hostility between men and animals will cease. Hostility between nations will cease; the Davidic king will not rule the world; he will be the ruler only over Israel but will be a model of justice, humility, and righteousness for all nations. A part of this vision is the concept of universal history, the belief that all humankind will return to God and there will no longer be enmity between human persons or between God and humankind.

It is impossible in this short section for us to discuss in detail this total book. We have focused upon his early ministry as found in chapters 1 through 12. Let us now look at his final years. The material for this period is found in chapters 28 through 33. At this time Isaiah was speaking to the political situation when Hezekiah made his second attempt to revolt against foreign domination through support from Egypt. Hezekiah's attempt failed, and he was forced to submit. In this period Isaiah thunders forth his words of judgment against human pride. Yet again he offers hope if they return.

> For thus said the Lord God, the Holy One of Israel,
>   "In returning and rest you shall be saved;
>   in quietness and in trust shall be your strength."
> And you would not.
>
> —Isaiah 30:15

Isaiah is the prophet par excellence. In him the meaning of Israel's faith reaches its zenith; Isaiah brought a message which focused upon a God who was lord of all history. God governs the earth with his providential care. He is sole sovereign of all the world. God's judgment is a manifestation of his power. Through it he confronts persons with their moral sinfulness. He calls for justice and righteousness, not empty sacrifice. Isaiah presents a vision of this God who will bring in a day of peace and joy for all. Isaiah's message was shared by Jeremiah, known as the "weeping prophet."

Jeremiah

Jeremiah's career spanned over four decades during the reigns of the last kings of Judah: Josiah (640–609 B.C.), Jehoiakim (609–598 B.C.), and Jehoinchin (598–597 B.C.). His ministry can be divided into four periods in which he sought to give some understanding to the crucial events that were making their impact upon Israel.

Jeremiah was born in a priestly family in Anathoth, northeast of Jerusalem and very early became aware of a special call.

> Now the word of the Lord came to me saying,
> "Before I formed you in the womb I knew you,
> and before you were born I consecrated you;
> I appointed you a prophet to the nations."
> —Jeremiah 1:4-5

His early ministry took place before Josiah's reformation was completed (626-622 B.C.). He had a brief ministry in Anathoth and then went to Jerusalem and attacked the cultic, ethical, and political sins of his people. Several passages indicate the condition of the people. First, they had a sense of false security (Jeremiah 5:12-13; cf. Jeremiah 6:28-30). In the midst of this situation, the prophet had one message:

> Go, and proclaim these words toward the north, and say,
> "Return, faithless Israel, says the Lord.
> I will not look on you in anger,
>   for I am merciful, says the Lord;
> I will not be angry for ever."
> —Jeremiah 3:12

Nevertheless, Jeremiah was aware that his people would not respond, and therefore he had no alternative but to proclaim the wrath of God (Jeremiah 3:5-8; 6:10-12). This note of doom ends the first stage of Jeremiah's ministry.

The second stage comes during the reign of Jehoiakim (Jeremiah 7:1-20:18). This was a time when Jeremiah confronted the temple and the cult and had serious conflicts with Jehoiakim. Jeremiah's attacks on the temple and the cult were based upon his conviction that sacrifices are not the core of religion; they can never be the substitute for fulfilling the divine will (Jeremiah 7:21-28). Jeremiah's thesis is that devotion of the heart is integral to any external practices or sacrifices.

Jeremiah not only attacked the temple and the cult. He also predicted the Exile and thereby evoked the wrath of not only the temple leaders but also the officials (cf. Jeremiah 13:15-27). This stance forced the high priest Pashhur to beat Jeremiah, and he was put in stocks (Jeremiah 20:2). This imprisonment did not stop Jeremiah. He felt that the divine urgency forced him to continue his prophecy in spite of his personal struggle.

This conviction forced Jeremiah to continue his prophecy during the reign of Zedekiah, the third period of his work. Jeremiah reiterated the divine claims and attacked the kings and Babylonian party and nationalistic prophets. As a result of this attack they threatened Jeremiah's life (Jeremiah 37–38).

In spite of his constant pronouncements against his people, he was constantly reminded that God cared (Jeremiah 23:1-8). Jeremiah had already seen this hope through his visit to the potter's house (Jeremiah 18:1-12). This made him aware that in spite of the calamity God's presence would still be with his people. On the basis of his faith he proclaimed:

> "Behold, the days are coming, says the Lord, when I will make a new covenant with the house of Israel and the house of Judah, not like the covenant which I made with their fathers when I took them by the hand to bring them out of the land of Egypt, my covenant which they broke, though I was their husband, says the Lord. But this is the covenant which I will make with the house of Israel after those days, says the Lord: I will put my law within them, and I will write it upon their hearts; and I will be their God, and they shall be my people. And no longer shall each man teach his neighbor and each his brother, saying, 'Know the Lord,' for they shall all know me, from the least of them to the greatest, says the Lord; for I will forgive their iniquity, and I will remember their sin no more" (Jeremiah 31:31-34).

This is a classic text in the Old Testament. In spite of the impending doom that Jeremiah saw overtaking his country, he could offer the promise of a new day. Fohrer is helpful when he argues that the word "covenant" really should be translated as "obligation." It is the obligation that one imposes upon oneself, upon another, or that a person arrives at by mutual consent with another person. It is in this sense that we can understand Jeremiah's letter to the exiles. This is the sense of ought—the obligation imposed upon oneself that Jeremiah expressed in the new covenant. Commitment to God is not only expressed by external acts of piety and sacrifice but also through unconditional commitment to God. Jeremiah lived by this principle. Because of this and his other prophetic acts, he was deported.[6]

Jeremiah was forced to accompany a group of refugees after the fall of Jerusalem (chapters 42–43). This was the fourth period of his ministry. This stage was brief. To the end he emphasized God's judgment, but also his care for Israel. He, like the prophets Amos, Isaiah, Micah, Nahum, Zephaniah, and Habakkuk, presented an understanding of the experience of the Israelites during this period and pronounced God's judgment undergirded with love. What do the messages of these prophets say to us today?

THE CROSSING POINT

The story is told of an Indian tribe that followed the custom that the smartest person in the tribe ruled as chief. If, at any time, the chief could be outwitted, the person who demonstrated such wisdom would automatically become the new chief.

A young, ambitious brave felt that he had a plan that would outsmart the ruling chief. Therefore, he requested an audience with the chief and presented himself before the chief with a small bird hidden in his hand. He thought, "I will ask the chief a question, 'Do I have in my hand life or death?'" If the chief replied, 'You have life in your hand,' he would immediately squeeze the bird to death and reply, 'No, I have death in my hand.' On the other hand, if the chief said, 'You have death in your hand,' the young brave had decided that he would open his hand and let the bird fly freely before them, obviously alive. What the young brave did not count on was the ability of the wise chief to observe that a part of the bird's tail protruded out of his hand. The chief was able to assess the situation immediately; so when the brave asked his tricky question "Do I have in my hand life or death?", the sagacious chief exclaimed, "You have both life and death in your hand!"

This was what the prophets were saying to Israel: God is the Creator and Judge; he has called Israel to be his people. God has given you the Law and the temple as the basis of his covenant. You can obey him and live—or you can disobey him and die. Judgment is imminent if you refuse, but peace and mercy are available if you obey.

Even though you have sinned, if you repent, God will have mercy on you and save you from destruction. You have in your hand life and death!

This was the burning message of the prophets. It speaks to us today with the freshness of the morning dew. The crossing point between the message of the prophets and our faith today is clear. We are called to understand God's call to decision.

Whereas the call in Israel's day came from the context of Israel's history, our call comes from twenty centuries of Christian history with the incarnation of Jesus Christ being the message. In the legacy of the prophet, Christ calls us with the challenge "You have in your hands life and death," or as Jesus put it, "Come to me, all who labor and are heavy laden, and I will give you rest. Take my yoke upon you, and learn from me; for I am gentle and lowly in heart, and you will find rest for your souls. For my yoke is easy, and my burden is light" (Matthew 11:28-30).

This call of the prophet to repent contains significant insights for our understanding of the nature of the relationship between God and humankind.

First, the call to decision was based upon the nature of God. God was holy and righteous. Those who followed him must reflect his holiness and righteousness.

Second, this call is necessary because religion is not primarily liturgical or cultic, but moral. Religion is not primarily one's cultic behavior, but one's commitment to reflect the attributes of God in love of neighbor and self. Social morality which emphasizes justice and mercy is the keystone of faith.

This message is the core of faith today. Faith in God requires fidelity to his nature. Jesus dramatized this concept of morality when he stated:

Jesus answered, "The first is, 'Hear, O Israel: The Lord our God, the Lord is one; and you shall love the Lord your God with all your heart, and with all your soul, and with all your mind, and with all your strength.' The second is this, 'You shall love your neighbor as yourself.' There is no other commandment greater than these" (Mark 12:29-31).

Third, the God who is holy and who is just is also merciful. The prophetic message, though full with judgment, always included the hope that Israel would repent.

We have in our hand life and death because God is merciful. Yes, we deserve death—we deserve judgment, but God offers mercy if we repent. In the historical experience of Israel judgment came. The Exile was a reality. Both the Northern Kingdom and the Southern Kingdom came to a calamitous end, but the prophets saw beyond these events and proclaimed God's mercy in spite of Israel's turning away from him.

This is the meaning of the "incarnation." It is God's word of love— it is his declaration. In his mercy he forgives those who come to him.

God's mercy is demonstrated in the parable which we find in Luke 15:11-24. Helmut Thielicke suggests that we call this "The Parable of the Waiting Father." The critical part of this text states: "And he arose and came to his father. But while he was yet at a distance, his father saw him and had compassion, and ran and embraced him and kissed him" (Luke 15:20). This is the God of mercy—the God of the prophets—the God of Jesus Christ who awaits our return. God is holy and righteous. God demands our faithfulness, but he is also merciful!

QUESTIONS FOR FURTHER CONSIDERATION

- In what sense is the story of "the prodigal" manifested in our daily lives?
- In what way are we alienated from God?
- How do we evaluate our response to the messages from God?
- Is God's messenger no more than an orator? Or is he/she a guide?

The Exile
and Restoration
Chapter 9

A. W. O'Shaughnessy has aptly described the period of the Exile and the return in the following phrase, "For each age is an age that is dying. Or one that is coming to birth." [1] The experiences of the Israelites during the Exile indicate that it was the age that was dying: destruction, corruption, judgment. At the same time it was an age that was coming to birth, through restoration. The temple was being rebuilt, the land restored, and the exiles returned to reaffirm their obedience to God. This was really an "age on age."

This period has all the dynamic interrelationships which make life challenging and invigorating. Although this period involved the Hebrew nation, it speaks also to our individual lives. Our lives are a constant cycle of dying and being reborn. We are always caught in the interplay between yesterday, today, and tomorrow. It was the undergirding power of God that enabled the despairing and dejected exiles to return from the Exile and begin anew; such an example of the power of faith is our model for today. Their story is the theme of this chapter.

The purpose of this chapter is to treat the experience of the Israelites in the period of the Exile and the restoration. On the basis of the Hebrew understanding, we can reflect upon their relevance for us today. Let us look first at the experience and understanding of the Exile which took place following the fall of Jerusalem and Judah.

THE EXILE
The Experience

There were at least four results of the fall of Jerusalem. (1) The temple was destroyed; (2) the dynasty of David came to a disastrous end; (3) the offering of sacrifices ended; and (4) the population was decimated, either by execution or deportation. The destruction of Jerusalem and the general devastation that followed are pictured in the five oracles by an apparent eyewitness of the fall of Jerusalem. One oracle depicted the dismal scene:

> How lonely sits the city
>   that was full of people!
> How like a widow has she become,
>   she that was great among the nations!
> She that was a princess among the cities
>   has become a vassal.
>
> —Lamentations 1:1

Although the focus of the biblical texts was upon the destruction of Jerusalem and the deportation of the cream of the crop, one should not assume that all the people left the city. The removal of the leading citizens made it possible for the poor of the land to assume control of the government through Babylonian appointments. Yet for the biblical writers the most important scene was in Babylon where many of the Jews were exiled and dispersed.

The Jews in the Exile were in partial captivity. They apparently had limited freedom and engaged in normal agricultural work. They ordered their affairs with little external interference. This limited freedom does not deny the fact that for the exiles Babylon was an oppressive situation. The psalmist says that they hung their harps upon the willow trees.

> By the waters of Babylon,
>   there we sat down and wept,
> when we remembered Zion.
> On the willows there
>   we hung up our lyres.
> For there our captors
>   required of us songs,
> and our tormentors, mirth, saying,
>   "Sing us one of the songs of Zion!"
>
> How shall we sing the Lord's song
>   in a foreign land?
>
> —Psalm 137:1-4

Restriction of freedom dehumanizes the individual and thwarts growth. This condition in Babylon severely challenged Israel's religious life. Many defected from the faith; others worshiped the Babylonian gods along with God (Ezekiel 14:1-11). The most significant contribution to Israel's religion came through those who took the situation as the time to reflect more deeply upon the meaning of their faith in God. This group developed the religious school, the prototype of the synagogue, to replace the temple. In these schools people heard lectures and worshiped with hymns and prayers. In the absence of a temple only a few of the cultic practices were continued, such as circumcision, fasting, and ancient dietary regulations. The adoption of these practices, which grew out of the practical necessity, became a reason for the Jewish exclusivism that emerged in the period following the exiles. The books of Ruth and Jonah were written later to counteract this tendency. In addition, these religious schools and cultic observances tended to separate the Jews from the Babylonians and led to the intensification of the legalism that was expressed in the Deuteronomistic reformation: the law became the substitute for the cult. Nevertheless, this development had a positive note. These practices established the basis for a clear understanding of what was happening to them in this period. They were able to affirm trust in his promise of deliverance. This faith undergirded them.

The Understanding

Jeremiah, Ezekiel, and the latter part of the book of Isaiah help us to understand the experience of this period.

Jeremiah

Jeremiah was the first of the classical prophets to be an eyewitness to the fall of Jerusalem in 587 B.C. This event was in fulfillment of the doom which Jeremiah had constantly predicted. Jeremiah's understanding was that Judah's destruction was due to several factors: namely, (1) the unfaithfulness of Judah to her obligation to God, (2) Judah's insensitivity to the fate of the Northern Kingdom, and (3) the religious and social corruption that characterized Judah's religious and political practices although Jeremiah issued warnings and summoned them to repentance (Jeremiah 26–27; 32–36; 37–44).

Undergirding these summons to repentance, Jeremiah promised deliverance. Two passages addressed to the exiles who were deported in 597 B.C. illlustrate this hope. In chapter 24 Jeremiah depicts the exiles, in the vision of the two baskets of figs, as good figs, and he promises restoration and renewal. Also in chapters 26 through 36 and 37 through 44, the exiles in Babylon are seen as holding the key to the future. Another passage which treats the theme of renewal is found in Jeremiah's symbolic action in which he buys back a parcel of land at Anathoth (Jeremiah 32:6-15). This passage suggests Jeremiah's understanding of this period. He saw recovery of life in Judah. The Exile was the purification rite for a renewed Judah. In Jeremiah, doom and revival are constant themes as he sought to understand God's activity in this crucial time in Israel's history.

Ezekiel

Ezekiel, the priest of Jerusalem, shared this understanding of the Exile. He felt an urgent call to proclaim God's message in a time of crisis. The apocalyptic vision forms the structure of this book. It is the reason one commentator wrote, "No other book gives us a more sublime vision of the majesty of God."

This apocalyptic vision is characteristic of Ezekiel. He proclaimed his message in veiled language, but the basic message is unmistakable. God is in control of the universe, and God is calling his prophet to assure the people of this fact. For the expressed purpose of proclaiming God's glory and lordship Ezekiel was called (Ezekiel 2:1-10; 3:1-3). The theme of his early message was: Jerusalem will fall; its destruction is inevitable. The watchman must report what he sees.

And at the end of seven days, the word of the Lord came to me: "Son of man, I have made you a watchman for the house of Israel; whenever you hear a word from my mouth, you shall give them warning from me" (Ezekiel 3:16).

Yet Ezekiel in his role as watchman focused upon the community and the individual. The fall of Jerusalem and the impending doom are the result of the corporate past sins of the community. Yes! But the individuals are also responsible! When the exiles placed the blame upon their fathers, Ezekiel thundered back to them that they were personally culpable for their situation:

The word of the Lord came to me again: "What do you mean by repeating this proverb concerning the land of Israel, 'The fathers have eaten sour grapes, and the children's teeth are set on edge'? As I live, says the Lord God, this proverb shall no more be used by you in Israel. Behold, all souls are mine; the soul of the father as well as the soul of the son is mine: the soul that sins shall die" (Ezekiel 18:1-4).

This passage suggests a critical shift in the focus of his thinking. It foretells a fundamental understanding of future Jewish thought which found its way into the New Testament. The individual as well as the community stands before God for judgment and redemption.

Although Ezekiel realized that his mission was to the individual, he did not neglect to remind the community that Israel had a history of unfaithfulness to God. He was also worried that they were still rebellious and that the people would not respond (Ezekiel 3:4-11). This refusal on their part continued in their history which reflected nothing but perversity and disobedience (Ezekiel 20).

Nevertheless, Ezekiel picked up Hosea's message. God is like the divine shepherd who seeks out to save his sheep (Ezekiel 34). Also God promised that in spite of the fact that they felt like a group of bleached bones, God would renew the dead nation by his spirit (Ezckiel 37:1-4). The first text provides the motivation for God's act. In spite of Israel's sins past and present, individual and collective, God loves her. The second passage promises the divine activity on Israel's behalf. God will resuscitate the dry bones by his spirit. This resurrection will bring into being a new nation, a Holy Nation with the Holy Temple at the center of its life. The vision of the dry bones sets forth the hope of restoration.

The theme of restoration is a basic theme in Ezekiel's ministry. Although it was there all the time, it was more pronounced following the fall of Jerusalem. The theme of restoration begins in Ezekiel 20:33-34 and concludes with a picture of the holy mountain where Israel obeys and worships God:

"For on my holy mountain, the mountain height of Israel, says the Lord God, there all the house of Israel, all of them, shall serve me in the land; there I will accept them, and there I will require your contributions and the choicest of your gifts, with all your sacred offerings. As a pleasing odor I will accept you, when I bring you out from the peoples, and gather you out of the countries where you have been scattered; and I will manifest my holiness among you in the sight of the nations. And you shall know that I am the Lord, when I bring you into the land of Israel, the country which I swore to give to your fathers. And there you shall remember your ways and all the doings with which you have polluted yourselves; and you shall loathe yourselves for all the evils that you have committed. And you shall know that I am the Lord, when I deal with you for my name's sake, not according to your evil ways, nor according to your corrupt doings, O house of Israel, says the Lord God" (Ezekiel 20:40-44).

Deutero-Isaiah

In the foregoing discussion we focused upon Ezekiel's understanding of the Exile—doom was to come, sorrow would come—but God is Deliverer; he will redeem his people. Ezekiel's understanding was rooted in a profound faith in God as Lord of history. An unknown prophet called Deutero-Isaiah (Second Isaiah) developed this belief further in chapters 40–55 in the book of Isaiah.

It is generally agreed that there are vast differences in language, style, and focus between Isaiah 1–39, Isaiah 40–55, and Isaiah 56–66. Various suggestions have been made to explain these differences. The present author feels that the evidence is clear that the material in Isaiah 40–55 is addressed to the period of the Exile. This biblical writer seeks to interpret to the deportees the meaning of their situation in Babylon and seeks to lift their hopes to see a new day. Deutero-Isaiah's themes are: Babylon's downfall, the return of the exiles, the rebuilding of the city of Jerusalem and the temple, and the universal proclamation of the knowledge of God.

These themes are presented in a striking fashion.

> Comfort, comfort my people,
>   says your God.
> Speak tenderly to Jerusalem,
>   and cry to her
> that her warfare is ended,
>   that her iniquity is pardoned,

> that she has received from the Lord's hand
> double for all her sins.
> —Isaiah 40:1-2

Through divine inspiration the prophet announces God's acceptance of Israel's repentance and presents God's decision to redeem his people. Deutero-Isaiah presents God as the one God, Sovereign Lord of history. He is Creator of all things (Isaiah 40:12-26). In brilliant language the prophet proclaims the oneness of God.

> Thus says the Lord, the King of Israel
> and his Redeemer, the Lord of hosts:
> "I am the first and I am the last;
> besides me there is no god."
> —Isaiah 44:6 (cf. Isaiah 45:18, 22; Isaiah 46:9)

God is not just the God of Israel; he is Lord of the whole earth. These passages speak to the heart of the concept of God which emerged from the Exile. It is the belief that there is one God and one God alone. This concept denies the existence of any other God. These passages show the full bloom of Israel's faith. Just as the lily emerges in all of its idyllic beauty from the ugly slime of putrid water, so from the barrenness of the Exile emerges one of the most lofty concepts of God that one finds in the Old Testament. Yahweh is God and there is no other one besides him. This tremendous revelation forced the prophet to expand his horizons concerning the restoration.

The prophet goes even further than his fellow prophets who saw the restoration as a return of the exiles to their homeland and a revival of the Davidic state. Deutero-Isaiah saw the establishment of God's rule in the world. He declared that a "new thing was about to take place."

> "Behold, I am doing a new thing;
> now it springs forth, do you not perceive it?
> I will make a way in the wilderness,
> and rivers in the desert."
> —Isaiah 43:19 (cf. Isaiah 42:9; 48:3, 6-8)

Utilizing the Exodus theme, he saw the coming deliverance as a new exodus, far more glorious. The beginning of this new event stretches back to creation itself. As all persons were created by God, all will be redeemed by him. This new day will usher in the kingly ruler of God. The Exile and restoration from this perspective take on an entirely different meaning.

Deutero-Isaiah accepted the fact that the Exile was caused by Israel's sin. Yet he saw God using this experience to a greater end. The Exile and restoration provided a new mission, a new destiny for Israel. Her role is to witness to God's universal purpose in history and to his sovereignty as one true God. The author used the figure of the suffering servant to give meaning of this new destiny to the exiles in Babylon (Isaiah 53). However, for the Christian, Jesus is the suffering servant.

Yet Deutero-Isaiah identified Israel with this servant of God in that Israel was the recipient of salvation; Israel was called upon to proclaim God's salvation; and the servant had a ministry to the nations. In the context of the Exile, this meaning of the servant has real significance. Thus both the individual and the corporate understanding of the suffering servant are possible without any necessary conflict.

For the exiles, the message of the prophet was that they were to be mediators of the universal understanding of God's lordship and oneness. When Jesus came to the world, he understood his mission as the servant of God. Jesus quoted from this same prophet when he began his ministry in Nazareth.

"The Spirit of the Lord is upon me,
  because he has anointed me to preach good news to the poor.
He has sent me to proclaim release to the captives
  and recovering of sight to the blind,
  to set at liberty those who are oppressed,
  to proclaim the acceptable year of the Lord."
—Luke 4:18-19 (cf. Isaiah 58:6; 61:1-2)

Both the exiles and Jesus understood the challenge of the prophets. Deutero-Isaiah helped the exiles to understand their predicament. Instead of wallowing in their despair, they were challenged to new possibilities.

Howard Thurman tells the story of a term paper written by a student who was a scuba diver. The student pointed out that as one descends the watery depth, one experiences the darkness which increases as one proceeds downwards. Suddenly, unexpectedly, the darkness takes on a luminous quality; there is a light in the darkness! This is what Deutero-Isaiah became for the exiles: in the midst of their darkness while they were descending in despair, he came with a luminating word. God has not forsaken you! God is the Lord of history; he will redeem you. He has a new mission, a new destiny to which he is calling you!

THE RESTORATION

The theme of restoration which was proclaimed by the three prophets of the Exile was fulfilled when Cyrus, the king of Persia, came to power. His ascendancy to the throne came as a result of the decline of the dominating influence of Babylon. This decline was due to internal strife. Nabonidus, who came to power in 556 B.C., was the last neo-Babylonian ruler. His absenteeism from the capital, leaving his son Belshazzar in power, angered the priest of Marduk in that his absence from the capital prevented them from celebrating the annual New Year festivals. This intensified other negative feelings against the king and eroded his power.

The Experience

Cyrus came to power in this historical context. He revolted against Astyages, the Median king, and overcame the alliances of Nabonidus, Croesus, king of Lydia, and Amasis, king of Egypt. First, he conquered Lydia (546 B.C.) and then defeated Babylon (539 B.C.). This secured the throne for Cyrus. He reigned until 530 B.C. It was in the first year (538 B.C.) of his reign that he issued the edict which permitted the restoration of Jerusalem. The edict provided for the temple to be rebuilt with royal funds and for the return to Jerusalem of the gold and silver vessels taken from the temple (Ezra 6:3-5; cf. 1:2-4). This action by Cyrus brought joy and happiness to the exiles. They began to return to Jerusalem.

The records in Ezra and Nehemiah indicate that there were at least four stages of the return. The first group returned as a result of Cyrus's edict in 538 B.C. Apparently this was led by Sheshbazzar who began the building of the temple but was unable to finish because of opposition (Ezra 1:8-10; 5:16). There was a second return which was led by Zerubbabel and Joshua when Darius I (521–485 B.C.) was king. In spite of opposition (Ezra 4:1-6) they completed the temple under the encouragement of the prophets Haggai and Zechariah (Ezra 3:1-13). The third group to return was led by Nehemiah on two occasions while Artaxerxes II (464–423 B.C.) was on the throne. They had two purposes: to rebuild the walls and to reestablish the cultus. Opposition also arose against their attempt to build the city (Ezra 4:7-23). The fourth group to return was led by Ezra. He brought with him the Law of Moses.

The significance of Ezra for this study is Ezra's role in the codification of the Mosaic law. Ezra played a significant role during the restoration. Nevertheless, the idealism of the returning exiles came to a shocking halt. Instead of rain and a full harvest, they experienced drought and bad harvest; instead of a stable economy, they faced what modern-day economists would call inflation (Haggai 1:1-11). Instead of the people who remained welcoming them, the returning exiles were in constant friction. All of these internal trials were combined with the constant upheavals that were taking place among the aspirants for world power and domination. Into this period of chaos and transition the prophets and men of God tried to provide a perspective.

The Understanding

Haggai set the tone for this period. He continued the argument of the classical prophets: sin brings on punishment. Notably, the difference is that Haggai saw their failure to rebuild the temple as the particular cause. If they rebuilt the temple, their difficulties would end (Haggai 1:3-11). The people's attitude toward rebuilding the temple is expressed negatively (Haggai 1:2,4).

Haggai's emphasis upon the rebuilding called for more than the physical reconstruction. He understood the rebuilding to be symbolic of the people's attitude toward God (Haggai 1:2-11).

The rebuilding of the temple involved leadership. This is why Haggai in cooperation with Zechariah urged Zerubbabel to take the leadership. Zerubbabel was challenged to lead his generation to rebuild (Haggai 2:21-23). Over and over again, Haggai insisted that this was the time for rebuilding the temple for God's new age.

Zechariah, the contemporary of Haggai, had a similar understanding of this period. The building of the temple was God's opportunity to the returning exiles.

> Then he said to me, "This is the word of the Lord to Zerubbabel: Not by might, nor by power, but by my Spirit, says the Lord of hosts. What are you, O great mountain? Before Zerubbabel you shall become a plain; and he shall bring forward the top stone amid shouts of 'Grace, grace to it!'" Moreover the word of the Lord came to me, saying, "The hands of Zerubbabel have laid the foundation of this house; his hands shall also complete it. Then you will know that the Lord of hosts has sent me to you. For whoever has despised the day of small things shall rejoice, and shall see the **plummet in the hand of Zerubbabel**" (Zechariah 4:6-10; cf. Zechariah 6:9-15).

Zechariah saw the rebuilding of the temple as a prelude to the development of a new community and a new age. He utilized a different style to present his message. This included night visions and dialogues between God and himself with an angel serving as an interpreter. He used apocalyptic language similar to the type of language Ezekiel used. These messages consisted of eight visions which climaxed with the crowning of the messianic leader (Zechariah 6:9-15). The last verse summarizes the main message of these visions:

> "And those who are far off shall come and help to build the temple of the Lord; and you shall know that the Lord of hosts has sent me to you. And this shall come to pass, if you will diligently obey the voice of the Lord your God" (Zechariah 6:15).

The new age finally comes when the temple is built.

Another key interpreter of this period is the priestly writer(s) who edited the hexateuch from Genesis to Joshua. It contains most of the latter half of Exodus, all of Leviticus, most of Numbers, a small section in Deuteronomy, and several sections in Joshua. This writer(s) interpreted Israel's history from the liturgical perspective. Several important themes are found in this history. This view emphasized the holiness of God. Since God is holy, he requires Israel to be holy, to separate herself from any foreign commitments.

Israel's historical moments are treated in their liturgical significance. The feasts which were celebrated in a later period are shown to be related to the Exodus. The Exodus was God's call to Israel to be his holy people (Exodus 12:1-20). This call is the heart of the author's understanding of Israel's history. Thus, the author divided Israel's history into four periods which marked the meaning of God's covenant with Israel. These periods are: Creation of the world and Covenant of dominion (Genesis 1:1–2:4a); Deluge (Genesis 6:9–8:22) and second Covenant with Noah (Genesis 9:1-17); Abraham and circumcision (Genesis 17); Sinai (Exodus 19:1; 24:15b-18a; 25:1–31:17; 31:18a).[2] Undergirding these covenants was the priestly writer's belief that God was revealing himself to Israel and enabling Israel to develop the sacrificial worship required by him.

They believed that God's requirement to rebuild the temple was just and fair. They were convinced that the chaos and difficulties that the people experienced were justly due, because their failure to rebuild the temple reflected the deeper question of their trust in God. The understanding was made clear; the judgment was made—God was just. He must deal with both righteousness and wickedness. Righteousness merited reward; wickedness provoked punishment. Retribution is the word that helps us to understand the interpretation of this period; a return to God through the purification of cultic observances was seen as a way of reversing God's retributive judgments.

Retribution and the Nation

There are many passages in the Old Testament in which the concept of retribution is expressed (e.g., Joshua 7:12, 25; 1 Samuel 2:1-10; 3:13-14; 2 Chronicles 24:18). However, one of the most significant statements about retribution is found in Deuteronomy 28. Here, the biblical writer presents the concept of retribution in terms of "blessings" and "curses." Verses 1-14 present the "blessings": "And all these blessings shall come upon you and overtake you, if you obey the voice of the Lord your God" (Deuteronomy 28:2). Verses 15-68 present the "curses": "But if you will not obey the voice of the Lord your God or be careful to do all his commandments and his statutes which I command you this day, then all these curses shall come upon you and overtake you" (Deuteronomy 28:15; cf. Leviticus 26).

The concept of retribution is presented here as a guide toward understanding God's relationship to the people of Israel. God had established the covenant as the foundation of this relationship (cf. Exodus 34). If Israel adhered to the terms of the covenant, she would receive God's blessings; but if Israel violated the terms of the covenant, she would receive God's curses. Thus being warned of the consequences of their actions, the people of Israel were free to respond to the terms of their relationship with God in whatever way they chose.

This understanding of retribution was based upon God's relationship to Israel as a nation rather than to individuals as separate entities. Yet the individual's responsibility was not ignored by the community; each person was considered a responsible part of the community. Individual acts could bring either blessings or curses to the community (cf. the sin of Achan, Joshua 7). C. F. Whitley explains this relationship as the "indissoluble connexion of the individual with the community." He further states:

> Through it individual as well as communal suffering found explanation, while it was in turn the basis of the doctrine that Yahweh visited the sins of the fathers upon the children unto the third and fourth generation (Numbers 14:18).[3]

This belief in retribution was also used to explain the relationship between evil and suffering. Evil was the outgrowth of man's disobedience (cf. Genesis 3). Suffering was due to God's wrath. Walther Eichrodt makes this same point when he states:

> Basic to this struggle with the problem of evil, in Israel . . . was first the fact that the origin of suffering was held to be the displeasure and wrath of the Deity . . . this divine wrath was held to be due to the trespass of men. . . . God's wrath was . . . expressed chiefly in righteous retribution, which was the consequence of the violation of well-known laws; and it is this element of retribution which brought evil within the scheme of God's lordship over his people.[4]

Thus far, we have seen how the Hebrew understanding of retribution was primarily in terms of a national posture. However, the prophets Jeremiah and Ezekiel added a new dimension to the theme of retribution.

Retribution and the Individual

Both Jeremiah and Ezekiel, contemporary prophets during the Exile, emphasized the individual aspect of retribution. Both of them rejected the popular adage: "The fathers have eaten sour grapes, and the children's teeth are set on edge" (Jeremiah 31:29; Ezekiel 18:2). Jeremiah contended: "But every one shall die for his own sin; each man who eats sour grapes, his teeth shall be set on edge" (Jeremiah 31:30). Ezekiel concurred with Jeremiah. He exclaimed: "As I live, says the Lord God, this proverb shall no more be used by you in Israel. Behold, all souls are mine; the soul of the father as well as the soul of the son is mine: the soul that sins shall die" (Ezekiel 18:3-4). He continued his argument for individual retribution by emphasizing that each individual falls under the law of divine recompense:

"The soul that sins shall die. The son shall not suffer for the iniquity of the father, nor the father suffer for the iniquity of the son; the righteousness of the righteous shall be upon himself, and the wickedness of the wicked shall be upon himself" (Ezekiel 18:20).

Jeremiah and Ezekiel make the shift from the concept of communal retribution to individual retribution. They emphasize the responsibility of the individual for one's own acts. Israel made the judgment that her exile was a sterling illustration of the retributive principle. This awareness forced them to make a decision to repent and renew their allegiance to God.

THE CROSSING POINT

Two stories from World War II help to place in perspective the crossing point between the period of the Exile and contemporary living. The first story reveals an attitude toward tragedy and the second the response to a community tragedy.

Helmut Thielicke, the pastor of a church in Hamburg, Germany, relates the experience of his congregation during a bombing raid. The congregation was in worship when a bomb exploded near the church. The windows cracked and the plaster was shaken from the walls. The congregation, nevertheless, continued their service, and Thielicke spoke to them about the bombing experience. He sensed their despair and bewilderment: bombings, killings—war and all its ugliness. They persistently asked, "Why, God?" This pastor received the inspiration to speak God's Word to the congregation, but in doing so Thielicke spoke to all people. He explained to them that he could understand their agony and despair; he could understand their reason for asking

"Why?" But he suggested that another question was in order. From the ruins of their bomb-torn city, in the midst of their horrors and sorrows, although it was legitimate to ask "Why?", he suggested that they ask, "God, what are you teaching us from this time of crisis?"

This was for them a crossing point. The pastor of faith led his congregation in asking a different kind of question. The new question emerged from a different attitude. This was an attitude of trust. Thielicke led his congregation to say, "God, we do not know why these things are happening, but we trust that you know and that you have a message for us." Like the prophets in the Exile, they looked beyond their despair to the meaning of the experience. They asked expectantly, "God, what are you teaching us?"

While the British were bombing the Germans, the Germans were likewise bombing the British. One of the towns struck was Coventry, where the British had erected, many years previously, a magnificent cathedral. One of the tragedies of the bombing was the destruction of this cathedral! While visiting Coventry, this story was told:

On the morning after the cathedral was destroyed, the bishop and several members of the congregation went to the cathedral and beheld the ghastly sight. The roof had been blasted out; the stained-glass windows had been blown out; and the interior was scorched from the heat of the bomb. Only the altar remained in the midst of the charred ruins. Their first response was horror and disbelief. How could such a cathedral that had been so magnificently built and faithfully dedicated to the glory of God be destroyed by enemy forces? Like their German counterparts, they asked, "Why, God?"

The bishop was also shocked by this experience, but the presence of the altar inspired him. He took two pieces of charred wood from the ruins, made a cross, and issued a call for the congregation to worship on that very day in the midst of the ruins. His action suggested that God had given him a deeper understanding of what was going on. In spite of the bombing the congregation would meet and affirm "Praise God from whom all blessings flow!" Later that site was rebuilt. The cathedral established an outreach ministry not only for the people in Coventry, but in Germany as well.

The response of both of these congregations suggests the way God speaks to us, even in tragedy and despair. Not only is this true of nations, but also of individuals.

A young woman told of an experience in which God's Word spoke to her in a time of crisis. She had encountered severe losses and was on the brink of a nervous breakdown. One night she picked up the Bible and accidentally found Isaiah's message to the exiles:

> But they who wait for the Lord shall renew their strength,
>   they shall mount up with wings like eagles,
> they shall run and not be weary,
>   they shall walk and not faint.
>
> —Isaiah 40:31

She stated that tears began to run down her cheeks; the feeling of being burdened left immediately; and her mind which had been bewildered became surprisingly clear. She rejoiced that God was speaking to her in this experience. These are crossing points! To the Hebrews in exile, to the bomb-torn congregations of Hamburg and Coventry, to a young person in distress—they who wait on the Lord will renew their strength! From the ruins of the Exile we hear the words "Return to God!"

QUESTIONS FOR FURTHER CONSIDERATION

- How do we understand the postexilic theme of God's power to turn evil into good?
- Are we willing to have an attitude of hopeful waiting and an open interpretation of disaster?
- What is required to develop such an attitude?

Postexilic Judaism
Chapter 10

The poet Langston Hughes sets the perspective for our viewing the period which covered the four centuries prior to the birth of Christ:

Dream Deferred

What happens to a dream deferred?
  Does it dry up
like a raisin in the sun?
Or fester like a sore—
  And then run?
Does it stink like rotten meat?
Or crust and sugar over—
like a syrupy sweet?

Maybe it just sags
like a heavy load.

Or does it explode?[1]

Israel in this period experienced a dream deferred. The city of Jerusalem was still a rubble; the Jewish inhabitants were suffering from poverty and confusion. It was the winter of their "discontent." Those lofty dreams which they had had were now nightmares. A poet's question was a real one for Israel.

THE EXPERIENCE

We shall now move to the consideration of the experience of the Jews from 200 B.C. to 63 B.C. We might divide this history into three periods: the Hellenistic Age (332–175 B.C.); the Maccabean Rebellion (175–142 B.C.); and the Rule of the Hasmoneans (142–63

B.C.). Let us briefly review our early discussion of the Hebrew experience.

In 586 B.C. the independence of the Southern Kingdom came to an end. This tumultuous event was preceded by the split of the United Kingdom at the death of Solomon in the tenth century. The Northern Kingdom had been able to gain supremacy, but in 722, due to a series of complex causes both within and without, the Northern Kingdom fell before Sargon of Assyria. Approximately 136 years later, Judah (Southern Kingdom) suffered the same fate as she fell to the plunder of the Babylonians. The prophets saw that both Israel's and Judah's fall were God's judgment against Israel for her sins. Except for the brief Maccabean revolt, which temporarily restored independence (141-63 B.C.), the Jews never again had a government of their own which was not subject to alien authority until 1948 when the present state of Israel was established. Nevertheless, the Jews never lost their religious identity although they lost their land and state.

Although it was just a small country on the main communication line between the valley of the Nile and the land of the Euphrates and the Tigris rivers, Palestine became the battleground of great empires that sought to control her. Egyptians, Hittites, Syrians, Assyrians, and Babylonians fought for the possession of this Israel as she was subjected to the successive rule of the great empires of the Persians (538–332 B.C.), the Greeks (332–175 B.C.), and the Romans (63 B.C.– A.D. 395).

The experience of the Jews was shaped by these movements of foreign powers. The literature, though meager, attests to the fact that Judah was under constant harassment during the period 586–175 B.C., from the fall of Judah to the Maccabean revolt. We glean very little from Haggai, Zechariah 1–8, Nehemiah's memoirs, and possibly the book of Ezra. From Haggai and Zechariah we learn that the temple was rebuilt (520–516 B.C.) and that Zerubbabel, a descendant of David, was crowned as the king. However, Darius conquered all his enemies, removed Zerubbabel at once, although he granted to the Jews complete freedom in religious and cultural matters. With this freedom from external aggression and internal tumults the Jews were able to make the transition from kingdom to state and from state to holy congregation. There was increased emphasis on religion and the high priest became the head of Judaism, or as James Henry Breasted puts it, "The Jewish state was . . . a *religious* organization, a church with a priest at its head."[2] Thus the publication of the final edition of the Law of Moses (400 B.C.) was more important than the rebuilding of the temple (520–516 B.C.); the Law became the most vital original institution of Judaism.

In this period we see many Persian influences creeping in among the Jews. As a result, two paradoxical or contradictory tendencies appeared in Judaism. On the one hand, there was the work of Deutero-Isaiah who proclaimed that Yahweh was the only God in existence, hence his worship should be the only worship of the people (Isaiah 46:5-9). On the other hand, the apocalypses proclaimed the future subjection of all nations to the Jews.

> And this shall be the plague with which the Lord will smite all the peoples that wage war against Jerusalem: their flesh shall rot while they are still on their feet, their eyes shall rot in their sockets, and their tongues shall rot in their mouths (Zechariah 14:12).

In this context, law served to separate the Jews from the Gentiles. Morton Scott Enslin sees this as the result of "Persian dualism with its notions of the powers of good as personified in the Supreme Being in ceaseless clash with the forces of evil under their prince" of evil (the New Testament devil or Old Testament Satan).[3] Also, there developed the belief in future life with its recompenses and punishments.

These influences were not the conscious borrowings as much as what Enslin calls the " . . . almost imperceptible stimulation from forces which did not seem so strange. They were living in the world and simply went further than they knew."[4] This is the context in which the Jews lived their experience during this period.

We have reviewed briefly the experience of the Jews in this explosive postexilic period. We now look at the understanding that emerged in reflection upon these experiences.

THE UNDERSTANDING

The political and religious ferment which characterized this period was understood in similar fashion as the explanation which emerged during the Exile. First, they saw God at work, even in their turbulent history. Over and over again this theme was expressed in the books of Maccabees, especially Second Maccabees: God is Lord of history, he is kind, his power is over all:

> The prayer was to this effect:
> "O Lord, Lord God, Creator of all things, who art awe-inspiring and strong and just and merciful, who alone art King and art kind, who alone art bountiful, who alone art just and almighty and eternal, who dost rescue Israel from every evil, who didst choose the fathers and consecrate them" (2 Maccabees 1:24-25).

He dwells in the reconstructed temple (2 Maccabees 14:35-36). Judas and his brothers were pictured as saviors (1 Maccabees 9:21; 14:29) who were sent by God to judge (I Maccabees 9:58-73) and deliver Israel thereby restoring her ancient inheritance.

> But Simon gave him this reply: "We have neither taken foreign land nor seized foreign property, but only the inheritance of our fathers which at one time had been unjustly taken by our enemies. Now that we have the opportunity, we are firmly holding the inheritance of our fathers" (1 Maccabees 15:33-34).

Basic to this understanding was the development of a different literary tradition to interpret the experience of the Israelite. This is called apocalyptic writing. It is mentioned now in connection with Daniel's attempt to help in understanding this period. A most succinct definition is given by Carroll Stuhlmueller in his discussion of the postexilic period in the *Jerome Biblical Commentary:*

> Apocalyptic, then, can be briefly characterized as an exilic and post-exilic development of prophetic style, in which heavenly secrets about a cosmic struggle and eschatological victory are revealed in symbolic form and explained by angels to a seer who writes down his message under the pseudonym of some ancient personage.[5]

The best illustration of this type of literature that comes out of this period is the book of Daniel. The classic apocalyptic vision is stated in chapter 7:

> In the first year of Belshazzar king of Babylon, Daniel had a dream and visions of his head as he lay in his bed. Then he wrote down the dream, and told the sum of the matter. Daniel said, "I saw in my vision by night, and behold, the four winds of heaven were

stirring up the great sea. And four great beasts came up out of the sea, different from one another. The first was like a lion and had eagles' wings. Then as I looked its wings were plucked off, and it was lifted up from the ground and made to stand upon two feet like a man; and the mind of a man was given to it. And behold another beast, a second one, like a bear. It was raised up on one side; it had three ribs in its mouth between its teeth; and it was told, 'Arise, devour much flesh.' After this I looked, and lo, another, like a leopard, with four wings of a bird on its back; and the beast had four heads; and dominion was given to it. After this I saw in the night visions, and behold, a fourth beast, terrible and dreadful and exceedingly strong; and it had great iron teeth; it devoured and broke in pieces, and stamped the residue with its feet. It was different from all the beasts that were before it; and it had ten horns. I considered the horns, and behold, there came up among them another horn, a little one, before which three of the first horns were plucked up by the roots; and behold, in this horn were eyes like the eyes of a man, and a mouth speaking great things" (Daniel 7:1-8).

This apocalyptic vision stands for the four successive empires of the Babylonians, Medes, the Persians, and the Greeks. The message is clear—these kingdoms will be battered and God's kingdom will emerge. This is the understanding that undergirded Israel's reflections upon this period.

In the assurance of God's rule of history, the people of Israel saw their role as patient and faithful children of God. Two stories illustrate this understanding. One refers to the friends of Daniel. The first story depicts the faithfulness of Daniel's friends—Shadrach, Meshach, and Abednego. They submitted themselves to a fiery furnace rather than bow down before an image of Nebuchadnezzar (Daniel 3:8-23). The message is clear: trust God, remain faithful, and he will be present with you in the time of need.

The second story is similar in its thrust and is about Daniel himself. Some of Daniel's fellow administrators envied him and sought a pretext to destroy him. They decided to exploit the fact that he prayed constantly to God. They had the king agree that no request would be made except to him. However, Daniel still prayed:

When Daniel knew that the document had been signed, he went to his house where he had windows in his upper chamber open toward Jerusalem; and he got down upon his knees three times a day and prayed and gave thanks before his God, as he had done previously (Daniel 6:10).

His enemies, spying upon him, reported this to the king who in turn threw him in the lion's den. However, Daniel was spared by God's power:

Then the king went to his palace, and spent the night fasting; no diversions were brought to him, and sleep fled from him.
    Then, at break of day, the king arose and went in haste to the den of lions. When he came near to the den where Daniel was, he cried out in a tone of anguish and said to Daniel, "O Daniel, servant of the living God, has your God, whom you serve continually, been able to deliver you from the lions?" Then Daniel said to the king, "O king, live forever!" (Daniel 6:18-21).

The insight which this story illustrates is that faithfulness to God is rewarded.

Another aspect of the understanding of the people of Israel during this period was that faithfulness meant fidelity to the Law. It was their belief that, if they kept the Law, the disasters which befell them before and during the Exile would no longer happen. Thus the Jews instituted a rigid legal system predicated upon a rigid belief in the revelation of the Torah (Law) to Moses.

The Torah became central, and Moses was venerated as the first and only receiver of the Law. One early collection of Jewish writings called *Sayings of the Fathers* (Pirgê Aboth) reflects this Jewish understanding:

Moses received the Torah [the written and unwritten Law] from Sinai and delivered it to Joshua, and Joshua to the Elders, and the Elders to the Prophets, and the Prophets delivered it to the men of the Great Synagogue.

True religion was revealed to Moses and was transmitted intact in an unbroken chain of reliable witnesses. The idea was also prevalent that the revelation to Moses, the Pentateuch, remained unchanged. The Scriptures were felt to be completed by Ezra and the men of the Great Synagogue "after whom divine inspiration ceased forever." Fidelity to God through rigid adherence to the Torah became a cardinal principle of Judaism.

The concept of a revealed religion through an unbroken literary tradition was connected by Jewish tradition and modern criticism with the name of Ezra the priest who brought the Law of Moses with him when he returned from Babylonia. He was commissioned by the Babylonian authorities to investigate the conditions in Judea with the authority to proclaim and administer this Law among the Jews. Ezra became a scribe and gave leadership to the restoration of the Law. Both Ezra and Nehemiah joined together in reestablishing the Jewish community; Ezra became the champion of the Law; Nehemiah gave leadership to the rebuilding of the walls. The Law was read (Nehemiah 8) and a "solemn day of fasting and prayer was set aside; a solemn day of fasting and humiliation," with confession of the sins of their forefathers and their own, bound themselves by a covenant under the signature and seal of the notables, and for the whole community by oath and curse (Nehemiah 9–10). The understanding that undergirded this act was that the Law was the key to the restoration of Israel.

In the above discussion we have seen that Ezra for the Jews was the restorer of the Law. It was received in its entirety by Moses from the mouth of God and delivered by him from time to time to the people from Mount Sinai to the Plains of Moab. Ezra was considered a faithful transmitter of the Law, for not only had he read the Law in Hebrew but also he had taken pains that it should be understood by having it rendered orally into the vernacular Aramaic as it was read. This focus upon the Law was critical.

In Nehemiah 10:28-39 we see the pact which the notables and peoples entered into, to walk in God's laws which were given by Moses and to observe and do all the commandments of the Lord our God. Then follow obligations which they imposed upon themselves for which there was no prescription in the Law, such as a poll tax which gave a third of a shekel for the maintenance of the public cultus. Also other regulations were agreed upon which were assumed by leading men with whom Ezra associated himself when he says, "We imposed on ourselves obligations." This group of leading men might have been the origin of the idea of the body called the Great Synagogue Keneset ha-Gedolah (Great Assembly or Convention). In the same tradition, in Pirgê Aboth (*Sayings of the Fathers*) which traced the continuous tradition of the Law from Moses to the days of Shamma and Hillel we read, "The prophets transmitted it to the men of the Great Synagogue."

The men of the Great Synagogue were responsible for the completion of the collection of the sacred books of Ezekiel, Daniel, Esther, and the Twelve Prophets in which the group Haggai, Zechariah, and Malachi were appended to the early prophets. Those who were transmitters of the unwritten law were called Traditioners or Teachers. Their successors were the Amoraim or Expositors, those who taught the Law as formulated in the Mishna and discussed it with their colleagues and pupils. This branch or stage of study was called Talmud (Learning). The one who wrote down the Law was called a sofer or scribe.

The Great Synagogue made several corrections of Ezra or the Soferun. They prescribed benediction and prayers (in the daily prayer) and benedictions ushering in holy time or marking its close (Kiddush and Habdalah). They authorized the observance of the Feast of Purim and fixed the days that were to be kept. Also, some thought that they prescribed the curriculum of study in the three chief branches of Jewish learning: Midrash, Halakah, and Haggadah. The motto of the men of the Great Synagogue in Aboth (Sayings) 1:1 is "Be deliberate in giving judgment and raise up many disciples and make a barrier about the Law." The first two clauses of *Sayings of the Fathers* address them as judges and teachers of the Law; the third is addressed to them as makers of the Law.

The scribes had authority to regulate the law. One of the last survivors of the Great Synagogue was Simeon the Righteous who, according to Jewish chronology, is the high priest who met Alexander the Great. Simeon's memorable word was, "The world rests on three pillars, on the Torah, on the cultus, and on the works of charity" (Aboth 1, 2). These may be paraphrased: knowledge of the divine revelation, the worship of God, and deeds of loving-kindness. These sentences are recognized fundamentals of Judaism.

"Antigonus of Socho, who received the traditional law from Simeon, said: 'Be not like slaves who serve their masters with the expectation of receiving a gratuity; but be like slaves who serve their master without expectation of receiving a gratuity; and let the fear of

Heaven be upon you'. . . . duty should be done for God's sake, or for its own sake . . . not for the reward of obedience. 'The man who fears the Lord delights greatly in His commandments' (Psalm 112:1)."[6] The delight is in the commandments, not in any reward for keeping them.

Let us look at the character of Judaism. Moore states:

> Of all the religions which at the beginning of the Christian era flourished in the Roman and Parthian empires Judaism alone has survived . . . because it succeeded in achieving a unity of belief and observance among the Jews in all their wide dispersion then and since.[7]

The Jews maintained the same system of dietary law; the synagogue had the same form of service with minor variations. Their prayers (Shema and Tefillah) could be said in any language. Hebrew seems to have been generally used wherever the Palestinian example was followed.

Although there was not a definite orthodoxy in theology as the basis for their unity and universality, the same authorities who regulated the observances also regulated the Jewish fundamental principle of its religious ethics and exemplified its characteristic piety. Some of these fundamental beliefs are:

1. Religion is revealed. God has made known what persons are to believe concerning themselves and others. Specific commandments were given to Adam, Noah, Abraham, and Jacob; to Moses complete revelation was given for once and for all. The prophets who came after him repeated, explained, emphasized, and applied what was revealed to Moses. This revelation to Moses was in part embodied in writing in the Pentateuch, in part transmitted orally from generation to generation in unbroken succession down to schools of law in which this tradition was defined, formulated, and systematized. Thus, the whole of religion was revealed; "Nothing was hidden"; the totality of revelation was religion.

2. There could be but one religion properly deserving the name of God, for God is One and revelation was consistent because God is One. The sin of the forefathers was not only that they worshiped other gods but also that they worshiped God in heathenish ways permitting injustice and immorality.

3. Sin required repentance. The people were responsible for the evils—individual, social, and political. They needed a religious and moral reformation in which the whole people must turn from evil

ways to God. The catastrophe of the Exile was the proof of this.

4. Retribution was individual, as well as corporate. Ezekiel and Jeremiah individualized the doctrine of retribution. Retribution is the belief that God blesses those who obey his will and punishes those who transgress or ignore his will. Ezekiel stressed the need for repentance as the sole but all sufficient ground for remission of all former offenses of the individual, just as earlier prophets from Hosea on had stressed retribution in relationship to the nation (Ezekiel 18; Hosea 14:2-10).

The Book of Job is a classic illustration of the problem of retribution. If suffering was due to sin, then how does one explain the suffering of an apparently righteous person?

5. Personal salvation was emphasized as a way of appropriating the doctrine of retribution. The interpreters of the Law taught that promises for divine forgiveness attached to the prescribed sacrifices and expiations, including those of the Day of Atonement, contain the implicit condition of repentance and when sacrifices and expiations ceased with the destruction of the temple, that repentance itself sufficed. In this way Religion became an I-Thou personal relationship between the individual and God.

6. The synagogue was the place where prayers were said together and individuals offered their private petitions, where the Scripture was read, interpreted, and expounded, a place of religious instruction and edification. This was a unique institution with the primary purpose of educating a whole people in its religion. Also religion and education found their center in the home. The people were taught to read and write. Josephus mentions as a generally known fact that the Torah made it incumbent to teach children to read and write, that they should know the Law (Torah) and be told of the deeds of their fathers. There were two schools (probably developed in the Maccabean period): the elementary school (Beth-ha-sofer) and a more advanced school or college (Beth-ha-Midrash). These colleges were intended for the expounding of the Torah.

The idea of God was lofty and noble. Although we see influences of contemporary philosophy in some Hellenistic writings, such as the Wisdom of Solomon, four Maccabees, and Philo, these are not in agreement with normative Judaism. Also, the Zoroastrian tendency to exempt God from the responsibility for evil by the attributing of the latter to another power was rejected because of the heresy of the two powers. Monotheism identified the moral order in the history with the will and purpose of God. Some claim that monotheism came out of the crisis of the Babylonian captivity.

The concept of God was so high that the people of Israel dared not speak the holy name (Yahweh) and it was announced by name only by the priest on the Day of Atonement only.

Where Yahweh was written, they read *adonay* ("My Lord"). They made even sparing use of this name and used heaven as in the Matthean formula (the kingdom of heaven). Also God was called Shekina, a "divine presence" from the temple "where his name was caused to dwell (like rays of sun)." It is the first hypostasis of the Godhead; it was the first step toward a Trinity.

God's power was absolute and nothing could thwart his power. He was omniscient and his presence was everywhere. He was wholly righteous and could not abide unrighteousness. Yet he was merciful, compassionate, and long-suffering. He had two moral attributes of mercy and justice.

Judaism stressed God as Father, or as Philo used it, "Father and Maker." This designation suggested that God's love was constant, and although his people rebelled, they were still his children.

In order to respond to God's love, the Jews insisted upon obedience to the Torah instruction. "Thou shalt love the Lord thy God" had the corollary "Thou shalt love thy neighbor as thyself." This included the stranger as well as the neighbor and kinsperson. Any violation of the Law was considered sin. Sin was defined in at least three categories: rebellion against God's authority in doing what is expressly forbidden; missing the mark; iniquity or moral distortion or crookedness.

Although the prophets depicted a golden age and restoration of the reign of David, postexilic Judaism widened this concept into the expectation of a day when the sovereignty of God would be acknowledged by all humankind when "the Lord shall be king over all the earth." In this view the conversion of the non-Jew was expected.

The belief in retribution took the form that at the end of the present age there would be a universal judgment. Hard times and crises sharpened this belief. Punishment would be universal on the Day of the Lord; the whole world would be judged. Famine, drought, war, and moral corruption of individuals would signify this day. These events would be birth pangs for the coming of the Messiah who would introduce the messianic age. Then the Messiah would come. We find the reactions to these messianic ideas in the New Testament. The Sadducees rejected it because they saw no basis for it in the Scriptures. The Pharisees were zealous for it and the Zealots wanted to rush it into fulfillment. Differing views of the "messianic age" continued into the New Testament period.

A summary of this character of Judaism might be found when Moore states:

> Judaism thus made religion in every sphere a personal relation between the individual man and God [I-Thou], and in bringing this to clear consciousness and drawing its consequences lies its most significant advance beyond the older religion of Israel. It was, however, a relation of the individual to God, not in isolation, but in the fellowship of the religious community and, ideally, of the whole Jewish people, the *Keneset Israel*.[8]

This discussion of Judaism is significant because it helps us to understand why the Old Testament is part of the church's book of faith. Most of these basic concepts of Judaism were operative when the Council of Rabbis met in Jamnia in A.D. 90 and selected the books that were to be included in the Old Testament. These ideas also were prevalent when Jesus was born. On both of these accounts we can see that the relevance of the Old Testament to the church's faith is greatly influenced by the ideas developed during this period following the exiles. Out of the disastrous experience of the Exile the Jewish people forged a religion whose flame we still see burning. Or to use another metaphor, after the deluge they developed a new covenant.

THE CROSSING POINT

This discussion of Israel's experience during the postexilic period has focused on the theme of a "dream deferred." The dream of an Israel returned to the glory of the days of David and Solomon exploded during the time of Judas Maccabaeus and his brothers. They believed that only violent revolution could restore Israel's glory.

The priestly writer(s) and his circle accepted the deferred dream but believed that the delay was caused by Israel's disregard of cultic purity. A rebuilding of the temple and a return to the Sabbath and festival observances and other cultic rites would ensure the fulfillment of the dream. Ezra and his followers also accepted that deferment of the dream, but they insisted upon strict adherence to the Mosaic tradition, as defined in the Torah, as the key to the fulfillment of the dream.

The prophets responded to the dream deferred with a view which stressed not so much Israel's future, but the future of humankind. They began to look not only at Israel's history but also at God's total control of history. From this perspective they saw that something more than cultic reforms and legal obedience was needed. God's future required an act far more radical than they imagined. They hoped for a new day! They hoped for a new understanding between God and humankind. They hoped for a world in which the lion and the lamb would lie down together.

As we seek to determine the crossing point between the postexilic period and our day, the prophets' concept of God's future for all of humankind speaks to us with enduring significance. Their emphasis upon the future and God's plan for history enables us to see that the hope has been fulfilled in Jesus Christ. We do not wait in vain for the fulfillment of our hope. We celebrate its coming in Jesus Christ through his birth, death, and resurrection.

In the play *Waiting for Godot,* two burned-out actors are portrayed as anxiously awaiting an appointment with a person named Mr. Godot. It is their hope that this person will open the door for them to renew their acting professions. At the end of the first act they are notified that Godot is delayed but that he is coming. This increased their enthusiasm and expectation. In the second act the two ex-actors still wait, but unfortunately the play ends without Godot ever appearing. They waited in vain.

This play has many possible interpretations, and many critics have presented theories on the meaning of it, especially Godot's name. The play suggests unfulfilled expectations. The actors waited for Godot, but the play also presents a perspective for examining the difference between the Jewish and Christian interpretation of the postexilic period. In Israel's experience Godot never came. Their hopes were not fulfilled. As Christians we believe that the postexilic hope has been fulfilled in the coming of Jesus Christ.

For both Jews and Christians hope is a significant aspect of human experience. It is a reaching out, a straining forward. Hope is an attitude of expectation, the sense that tomorrow will be better than today, the conviction that the Creator is still Lord of all history, and that despite the contingencies of evil and ambiguity, God will bring to fulfillment that which was begun in creation.

After the Exile Hebrews were convinced not only that God was the Creator, but also that he had called Israel into covenant relationship with himself. The turmoil and despair of the Exile and its aftermath were not in any way to be interpreted as God's rejection of Israel. No! God was purifying Israel. Keeping cultic vows and obedience to the Law were the necessary requirements for the renewal of the covenant. From this perspective we can see that the basis of their hope was the faithfulness of God to his covenant with Israel and his willingness to forgive Israel's infidelity to him. If Israel returned, God would have mercy and abundantly pardon. The fulfillment of the hope was not due to God's indifference but Israel's refusal to repent.

We Christians, too, affirm Israel's hope. We, too, believe that God is faithful to his covenant. But we believe that God has taken the initiative to forgive. The meaning of the incarnation is that our hopes are fulfilled in Jesus who comes to us in the midst of our sinfulness. Through him we receive pardon. God does not wait for us to fulfill all the cultic requirements or keep all the Laws. God set a new norm for the God-humankind relationship, that is, the acceptance of forgiveness through Jesus Christ.

This interpretation of Christian hope is found in the following New Testament Scripture. First, Paul states the ground of Christian hope:

> Now if Christ is preached as raised from the dead, how can some of you say that there is no resurrection of the dead? But if there is no resurrection of the dead, then Christ has not been raised; if Christ has not been raised, then our preaching is in vain and your faith is in vain. We are even found to be misrepresenting God, because we testified of God that he raised Christ, whom he did not raise if it is true that the dead are not raised. For if the dead are not raised, then Christ has not been raised. If Christ has not been raised, your faith is futile and you are still in your sins. Then those also who have fallen asleep in Christ have perished. If for this life only we have hoped in Christ, we are of all men most to be pitied (1 Corinthians 15:12-19).

Second, this fact of God's love in Christ brings us into a new relationship with God:

> There is therefore now no condemnation for those who are in Christ Jesus. For the law of the Spirit of life in Christ Jesus has set me free from the law of sin and death. For God has done what the law, weakened by the flesh, could not do: sending his own Son in the likeness of sinful flesh and for sin, he condemned sin in the flesh, in order that the just requirement of the law might be fulfilled in us, who walk not according to the flesh but according to the Spirit. For those who live according to the flesh set their minds on the things of the flesh, but those who live according to the Spirit set their minds on the things of the Spirit. To set the mind on the flesh is death, but to set the mind on the Spirit is life and peace. For the mind that is set on the flesh is hostile to God; it does not submit to God's law, indeed it cannot; and those who are in the flesh cannot please God (Romans 8:1-8).

God's action in Jesus Christ is the crossing point between Israel's postexilic experience and our faith today. We celebrate the coming of Christ as both the Creator and Guarantor of our hope!

QUESTIONS FOR FURTHER CONSIDERATION

- How does the Christian respond to the tension between eternal life and fear of death?
- How does the Christian cope with the sense of guilt and the need for goodness and forgiveness?
- In what sense can the Christian affirm that "Christ is the hope of the world"?

Notes

Chapter 1

[1]G. Ernest Wright, *God Who Acts* (London: SCM Press Ltd., 1952), pp. 33-58.

Chapter 2

[1]Paul Ricoeur, *The Symbolism of Evil,* trans. Emerson Buchanan (Boston: Beacon Press, 1967), p. 240.

Chapter 3

[1]Kierkegaard, quoted in Rollo May, *Man's Search for Himself* (New York: W. W. Norton Co., Inc., 1953), p. 10.

[2]*Ibid.,* pp. 138-142.

[3]Quoted in *ibid.,* p. 224.

[4]G. W. Anderson, *The History and Religion of Israel* (London: Oxford University Press, 1966), pp. 3-4.

[5]Georg Fohrer, *History of Israelite Religion,* trans. David E. Green (Nashville: Abingdon Press, 1972), p. 30.

[6]Theodore H. Robinson, "The History of Israel," *The Interpreter's Bible* (Nashville: Abingdon Press, 1952), vol. 1, p. 272.

Chapter 4

[1]Martin Noth, *The History of Israel* (New York: Harper & Row, Publishers, 1960), pp. 111-138.

[2]Martin Buber, *Moses* (London: East and West Library, published by Phaidon Press, Ltd., n.d.), p. 75.

[3]Noth, *op. cit.,* p. 137.

[4]J. Coert Rylaarsdam, "The Book of Exodus," *The Interpreter's Bible* (Nashville: Abingdon Press, 1952), vol. 1, p. 841.

[5]Gustavo Gutiérrez, *A Theology of Liberation,* trans. and ed. Sister Caridad Inda and John Eagleson (Maryknoll, N.Y.: Orbis Books, 1973), p. 155.

Chapter 5

[1]John Bright, *A History of Israel* (Philadelphia: The Westminster Press, 1959), pp. 124-127.

[2]John Bright, "The Book of Joshua," *The Interpreter's Bible* (Nashville: Abingdon Press, 1953), vol. 2, pp. 550 ff.

[3]Georg Fohrer, *Introduction to the Old Testament,* trans. David E. Green (Nashville: Abingdon Press, 1968), pp. 212-213.

Chapter 6

[1]Yehezkel Kaufmann, *The Religion of Israel,* trans. Moshe Greenberg (Chicago: The University of Chicago Press, 1960), p. 264.

[2]Henri J. M. Nouwen, *The Wounded Healer* (Garden City, N.Y.: Doubleday & Company, Inc., 1972), pp. 5-6.

Chapter 7

[1]John Philpot Curran, *The Oxford Dictionary of Quotations,* 2nd. edition (New York: Oxford University Press, 1955), p. 167.

[2]R. N. Whybray, *The Succession Narrative,* Studies in Biblical Theology, 2nd Series, No. 9 (Naperville, Ill.: Alec R. Allenson, Inc., 1968), pp. 54-55.

Chapter 8

[1]B. Davie Napier, *Song of the Vineyard* (New York: Harper & Row, Publishers, 1962), p. vi.

[2]Quoted by John Paterson, *The Goodly Fellowship of the Prophets* (New York: Charles Scribner's Sons, 1948), p. 47.

[3]Yehezkel Kaufmann, *The Religion of Israel,* trans. Moshe Greenberg (Chicago: The University of Chicago Press, 1960), p. 375.

[4]John Bright, *History of Israel* (Philadelphia: The Westminster Press, 1954), p. 273.

[5]Kaufmann, *op. cit.,* p. 387.

[6]Georg Fohrer, *Introduction to the Old Testament,* trans. David E. Green (Nashville: Abingdon Press, 1968), pp. 388-402.

Chapter 9

[1]Quoted by Arnold J. Tkacik, *Jerome Biblical Commentary,* ed. Raymond E. Brown (Englewood Cliffs, N.J.: Prentice-Hall, Inc., 1969), p. 344.

[2]Georg Fohrer, *Introduction to the Old Testament,* trans. David E. Green (Nashville: Abingdon Press, 1968), p. 180.

[3]C. F. Whitley, *The Genius of Ancient Israel* (Amsterdam: Philo Press, 1969), p. 104.

[4]Walther Eichrodt, *Man in the Old Testament.* Studies in Biblical Theology, trans. K. and R. Gregor Smith (London: SCM Press Ltd., 1951), p. 55.

Chapter 10

[1]Langston Hughes, "Dream Deferred," *On City Streets,* selected by Nancy Larrick (New York: M. Evans & Company, Inc., 1968), p. 149. Copyright 1951 by Langston Hughes. Reprinted from *The Panther and the Lash: Poems of Our Times,* by Langston Hughes, by permission of Alfred A. Knopf, Inc.

[2]James Henry Breasted, *Ancient Times* (New York: Ginn and Company, 1944), p. 235.

[3]Morton Scott Enslin, *Christian Beginnings* (New York: Harper & Row, Publishers, 1938), p. 5.

[4]*Ibid.,* pp. 5-6.

[5]Carroll Stuhlmueller, "Post Exilic Period: Spirit, Apocalyptic," *Jerome Biblical Commentary* (Englewood Cliffs, N.J.: Prentice-Hall, Inc., 1969), p. 343.

[6]Quoted by George Foot Moore, *Judaism* (Cambridge: Harvard University Press, 1932), vol. 1, p. 35.

[7]*Ibid.,* p. 110.

[8]*Ibid.,* p. 121.